91B 3
AF655366

SYNECTICS MODEL
OF
TEACHING

Synectics Model of Teaching

By

M.S. Talawar
G. Sheela

ANMOL PUBLICATIONS PVT. LTD.
NEW DELHI - 110 002 (INDIA)

ANMOL PUBLICATIONS PVT. LTD.
4374/4B, Ansari Road, Daryaganj
New Delhi - 110 002
Ph.: 23261597, 23278000
Visit us at: www.anmolpublications.com

Synectics Model of Teaching
© Authors
First Published, 2004

ISBN 81-261-2096-7

[All rights reserved. No part of this publication may be reproduced, stored in a retrieval system or transmitted, in any form or by any means, mechanical, photocopying, recording or otherwise, without prior written permission of the publisher.]

PRINTED IN INDIA

Published by J.L. Kumar for Anmol Publications Pvt. Ltd., New Delhi - 110 002 and Printed at Mehra Offset Press, Delhi.

Contents

Foreword

Today the world is progressing very rapidly. It is not possible to foresee how our lifestyles would be ten to fifteen years from now. What are the factors responsible for this rapid progress? It is the new invention and discoveries of man in the field of Science and Technology, Industry, Agriculture, Medicine. A handful of people who could think differently and ingeneously and who could offer new methods and solutions to problems are responsible for this progress. They are the creataive problem-solvers. They are invaluable assets to the society.

Where do these creative problem solvers emerge from? Certainly from our own society - through education. Children have a natural urge of inquisitiveness. But, this natural urge for creativity is hampered and dampened by our present classroom practices which emphasize on rigid convergent thinking.

According to Guilford (1957),"Education has emphasized abilities in the area of convergent thinking and evaluation, often at the expense of development in the area of divergent thinking. We have attempted to teach students how to arrive at correct answers that our civilization has taught us are correct. This is convergent thinking... Outside the arts we have generally discouraged the development of divergent thinking abilities unintentionally but effectively.

The aim of education is to nurture the child's capabilities to the fullest extent and to bring about all round development in the child. If this aim has to be realized then, "We will have to teach the child to think creatively about the yet-to-be discovered" (Crutchfield, 1967). Lowenfield and Britain (1966) said "To teach towards creativity is to teach toward the future of the society."

The development of creative problem solving ability among the adolescents is a major challenge in area of science education which needs to be tackled. Different strategies could be adopted by the teacher for this purpose.

This book aims at testing and showing how effective is Synectics Model of teaching in terms of fostering creativity and problem solving ability among secondary school students by adopting this model to teaching of science. The joint venture by Dr. M.S. Talawar, Dean, Faculty of Education and Dr. G. Sheela, Guest Faculty, Department of Education, Bangalore University deserve appreciation. This book is an outcome of intensive research work conducted by the authors. As such it is valuable for teacher-trainees, teacher educators, educational researchers, curriculum planners, policy makers and N.G.Os working for the cause of education.

I wish, the authors will work further so as to bring their knowledge and experience to the practical field and make education employable.

Dr. M.S. Thimmappa
Vice-Chancellor
Bangalore University

Preface

> *" Whether they serve in Governments or factories, hospitals or universities, villages or business houses, creative leaders are sorely needed by every society. Particularly in a developing country... they must take the lead. Clearly, creative men are urgently needed on every strata of society... Traditional societies must seek out, train and tangibly aid their potential innovators".*
>
> -McCord (1965)

Creative individuals are assets to any society. The discovery and development of creative genius of our youth should be the prime importance of our education. Children tend to be naturally creative, but their creativity is dampened as a result of authoritarian system of education. In the conventional method of teaching there is very little chance to discover and foster the creative potential of children. Science is natural for creativity. It is a creative venture into problem solving situations and new inventions. It is the product of creative thinking by scientists over a period of time.

Man's life is an endless stream of problems, situations for which an individual has no ready solutions. He requires to think and reason to solve a problem. Children possess an impressive array of thinking strategies. But they are inhibited from applying them in many classrooms. A considerable improvement in problem solving performance can occur when their responses are encouraged and accepted and the classroom atmosphere is made less threatening.

Creative individuals and good problem solvers are the cry of the hour. Teachers and educators, therefore have a great responsibility to children and society to see that these abilities are manifested to the maximum of the individual's potential. Special efforts are needed to develop creativity and problem solving ability among children through specially designed modes. Education is one of the potent instruments for development of creativity and problem solving ability, if it is properly geared for this purpose.

William, J.J.Gordon and his associates developed Synectics procedures to solve problems and invent new products in industrial settings. Analogies, which provide a bridge between a known concept and an unfamiliar concept, are chief elements in Synectics procedures. Synectics model of teaching is developed based on these procedures. It aims at creating learning environments in which creativity and problem solving ability of children could be fostered. There was a need to test its effectiveness in terms of developing creativity and problem solving ability. The present book is a result of this modest venture.

An introduction which provides fuel for thought to understand the study is provided in the first chapter. Studies related to different models of teaching, and variables considered in this study have been reviewed in chapter two. Chapter three presents the objectives, hypotheses and methodology followed for the study. Chapter four shows the analysis of data and its interpretation. You can have a quick bite of the whole study and the major findings in chapter five. The educational implications of the findings, which are the need of the day and the suggestions for further research which could be undertaken on related topics are presented in chapter six. Developing lesson plans based on Synectics model of teaching was an important aspect. Model lesson plans on Synectics model of teaching are presented in the appendix. Problem solving ability test developed by the Researcher is also being presented in the appendix.

We are deeply indebted to the Principal, Head Mistress and Teachers of Florence High School, Basaveshwaranagar, Bangalore for their cooperation and help in administering the tests and conducting the experiment. The cooperation and active participation of students, who are the pillars of this study is unforgettable.

We are deeply beholden to Dr. M.S. Thimappa, Hon'ble Vice-Chancellor, Bangalore University, for writing the Foreword to this book. We also thank Mr. J.L. Kumar, Managaing Director, and Shri V. Srinivasa Murthy, Resident Sales Executive (South), Anmol Publications Pvt. Ltd., New Delhi for their generous help to bring out this book at the earliest possible.

Our affectionate thanks are due to our family for their constant encouragement.

– Dr. M.S. Talawar & Dr. G. Sheela

1

INTRODUCTION
Fuel for Thought

Since the dawn of civilization, man has been curious to know the things around him. Man's search for truth is characterized by an appeal to custom, tradition, authority and personal experience and also to syllogistic reasoning. Man confronts nature compelling her to reveal her secrets and for that he makes systematic attempts. By his persistent efforts, careful experimentation and exact reasoning man has collected a mass of tested information, which we call science. And it is through education that this information or science is to be imparted to future generations, so that in future, knowledge grows on this information.

Education also builds ideas and emotions. Teaching and learning is such a wondrous and ever-changing process, wherein thoughts and feelings are built and rebuilt. The teachers arrange the learning environments, provide tasks, and try to learn what is going on in those wondrous and unique minds of children. Teaching is an adventure of learning about minds and how ideas and emotions interact with environments and become transformed. Venturing into this adventure, the educationists constructed models of teaching and learning that are built on the guesses they make about what is going on in those little minds.

Schools and classes are essential units of our society. They are communities of students brought together to explore the world and learn how to navigate it productively. We hope their members will understand their social world, be devoted to its improvement, and develop the dignity, self-esteem, and sense of efficacy to generate personal lives of high quality. These aspirations lead to the study of teaching and has resulted in the development of a rich array of models of teaching.

1.1 Models of Teaching

Teaching is more than presentation of facts. Teaching is the development of new ways of thinking - a development that reveals itself in increased skills with the problems of life, in new habits of action, in more desirable attitudes, in a benefited personality and in an improved character.

The main aim of teaching is to bring out socially desirable behavior change in the students and this can only be achieved if the teaching is effective. In India, efforts have been made to study classroom behavior of teachers with a view to identify teaching skills for the effective teaching of different subjects. Attempts are also made to find out teaching patterns which are conducive for developing cognitive abilities and effective behaviors in children.

It is generally agreed that the objectives to be achieved through the teaching learning process is multidimensional in nature. It is also known that no one particular method or technique is appropriate to achieve all these multi-dimensional objectives. This led researchers to explore the use of various methods and techniques in an integrated fashion which resulted in the development of new instructional strategies known as Models of teaching. A model of teaching is a plan or pattern that can be used to shape curriculum, to design instructional materials and to guide instruction in the classroom and other settings.

According to Bruce Joyce and Marsha Weil, models of teaching are also models of learning. Since they help students acquire information, ideas, skills, values, ways of thinking, and means of expressing themselves, they are also teaching them how to learn. The long term outcome of instruction is students' increased capabilities to learn more easily and effectively in the future, because of the knowledge and skill they have acquired and also because they have mastered learning processes. The way of teaching has a large impact on students' abilities to educate themselves. Successful teachers engage their students in robust cognitive and social tasks and teach the students how to use them productively. Outstanding teachers teach the students to learn. The effect of various models of teaching is measured not only by how well they achieve the specific objectives toward which they are directed (like self-esteem, social skill, information processing, ideas, creativity etc,.) but also by how well they increase the ability to learn, which is their fundamental purpose. Students will be able to accomplish more and more types of teaching more effectively as their repertoire of learning strategies increase.

The core of the teaching process is the arrangement of environments within which the students can interact and study how to learn (Dewey, 1916). A model of teaching is a description of a learning environment. The description may have many uses, planning curriculum, courses, units and lessons, to designing instructional materials like books, workbooks, multimedia programmes and computer assisted learning programme.

For more than 40 years Joyce and Weil (1980) conducted a continous and worldwide search for promising approaches to teaching and found models of teaching in abundance. These variety of approaches to teaching-learning were developed and followed by different learning theorists, philosophers, therapists and trainers in industrial, military and athletic settings. Based on them Joyce and Weil designed more than twenty five models of teaching. All have a coherent theoretical basis. Their creators provide the rationale and explain whey they expect them to achieve the goals for which they are designed. Through practice these models have been refined so that they can be used comfortably and efficiently in classroom and educational settings. These models of teaching have a great potentiality for achieving the aims and objectives of education. The models are grouped into four families viz.,

a) Information processing models

b) Social interaction models

c) Personal models

d) Behavior modification models.

a) Information processing models: emphasize the information processing capability of students and ways in which they can improve their ability to master information. 'Information processing' refers to ways people handle stimuli from the environment, organize data, sense problems, generate concepts, and find solutions to problems and employ verbal and nonverbal symbols. This family includes Inquiry Training Model, Inductive Thinking Model, Concept Attainment Model, Advance Organizer Model, Mnemonics Model, Cognitive Growth Model, Biological Science Inquiry Model and Synectics Model.

b) Social interaction models: emphasize the relationship of the individuals with the society and other persons. They focus on the process by which reality is socially negotiated. They give priority to the improvement of the individual's ability to relate to others, to engage in democratic processes and work productively in the society. Group Investigation Model, Social Inquiry Model, Jurisprudential Inquiry Model, Role Play Model, and Conceptual System Model come under this family.

c) Personal models: share an orientation towards the

individual and the development of self-hood. They attempt to shape education so that we come to understand ourselves better, take responsibility for our education and learn to reach beyond our current development to become stronger, more sensitive and more creative in our search for high quality lives. The personal models pay great attention to the individual perspective and seeks to encourage productive independence, so that people become increasingly self aware and responsible of their own destines. The models which belong to this family are Non-Directive Teaching Model, and Awareness Model.

d) Behavior modification models: have been designed drawing particularly on the work of B.F. Skinner. It has been designed to take advantage of the human being's capacity to learn and modify behavior by responding to tasks and feedback. These models are used to teach information, concepts and skills to increase comfort and relaxation and reduce phobias, to change habits and to help students engage social and academic tasks appropriately. The models of this family are Mastery teaching and Programmed Instruction, Anxiety Reduction Model, Simulation Model and Direct Teaching Model.

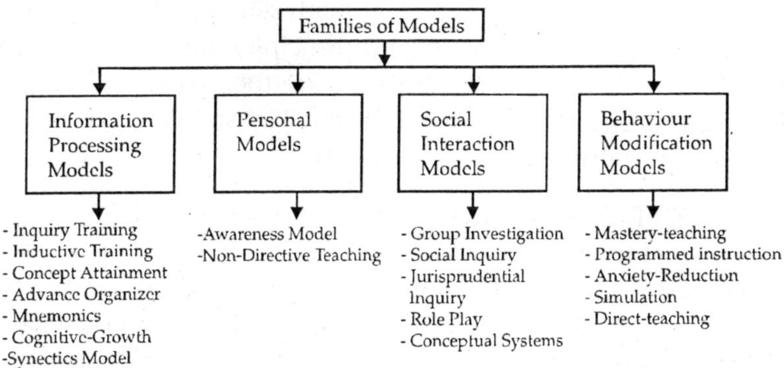

These families of models are not mutually exclusive. The actual prescriptions for developing the instructional activities and learning environments that emerge from some of them-even those classified in different families are remarkably similar. Also, within the families, models share many features with respect to goals and kinds of means they recommend. All educational activities evoke different meaning in different people, i.e., everything we do is personal. Similarly most of our experiences (especially educational ones) involve some intellectual or information processing activity. In general Bruce Joyce and Marsha Weil feel it is the basic framework of families that has become a powerful intellectual tool for teachers rather than the specific classification of individual models. However they made an effort to classify models according to the most prominent goal or features than distinguish them from another family. The models cannot be strictly categorized and claimed to develop abilities related to only personal development and not to information processing skills or social behaviour. Thus Synectics model of teaching which was grouped under personal family earlier has presently been shifted to information processing family.

The present study is focussed on the Synectics Model of the Information-Processing family.

Each model of teaching is analyzed in terms of four concepts: syntax, social system, principles of reaction, and support system. These descriptions are the operational heart of each model: they tell us what activities should occur and, when appropriate, in what sequence.

SYNTAX: The syntax or phasing of the model describes the model in action. For example, if the teachers were to use the model as the basis for their strategy, what kinds of activities would they use? How would they begin? What would happen next? Syntax is described in terms of sequences of activities called phases. Each model has a distinct flow of phases.

THE SOCIAL SYSTEM: The social system describes

student and teacher roles and relationships and the kind of norms that are encouraged.

PRINCIPLES OF REACTION: Principles of reaction tell the teacher how to regard the learner and how to respond to what the learner does. They provide the teacher with rules of thumb by which to tune in to the student and select model-appropriate responses to what the student does.

SUPPORT SYSTEM: It describes the supporting conditions necessary for the existence of a model. The additional requirements of the model beyond the usual human skills and capacities and technical facilities are being described. Support needed might be in the form of books, films, self-instructional systems, and travel arrangements if necessary.

INSTRUCTIONAL AND NURTURANT EFFECTS: The effect of an environment can be direct - designed to come from the content and skills on which the activities are based. Effects can also be implicit in the learning environment. The description of the effects of models can validly be categorized as the direct or instructional effects and the indirect or nurturant effects. The instructional effects are those directly achieved by leading the learner in certain directions. The nurturant effects come from experiencing the environment created by the model.

1.1.1 Synectics Model

The word Synectics derived from Greek means "the joining together of different and apparently irrelevant elements". Synectics theory applies to the integration of diverse individuals into a problem-stating problem-solving group. Synectics defines creative process as the mental activity in problem-stating, problem-solving situations where artistic or technical inventions are the result.

Synectics is an interesting approach to the development of creativity designed by William J.J. Gordon(1961). Synectics procedures were initially used to develop "creative groups" within industrial organizations - that is groups of persons trained to work together to function as problem solvers or product developers. But later Gordon adapted Synectics for use with school children. The chief element in Synectics is the use of analogies. Here the students "play" with analogies until they relax and begin to enjoy making more metaphoric comparisons.

Synectics is grounded on four ideas about creativity. These ideas that challenge the conventional views about creativity are:

i) Gordon views creativity as a part of our everyday activity. This is in contrast to the conventional idea where creative process is associated with the development of great works of art or music, or a new invention.

ii) Creative process is not mysterious. It can be described and people can be trained to increase their creativity. This is in contrast to the traditional view where creativity is viewed as a mysterious, innate and personal capacity that can be destroyed if its process are probed deeply. This view of Gordon that creativity is enhanced by conscious analysis led him to describe it and create training procedures that can be applied in schools and other settings.

iii) Creative invention is similar in all fields- the arts, the sciences, or engineering. The intellectual processes underlying it are the same. But commonly it is believed that creativity is confined to arts. In sciences it is called invention.

iv) Individuals and groups generate ideas and products in the same fashions. This is different from the conventional which views creativity as an intensly personal experience which could not be shared.

A set of assumptions about the psychology of creativity are used to develop specific processes of Synectics. The first assumption is that, by bringing the creative process to consciousness and by developing explicit aids to creativity, we can directly increase the creative capacity of both individuals and groups. The second assumption is that the "emotional component is more important than the intellectual, the irrational more important than the rational." The third assumption is that the "emotional, irrational elements must be understood in order to increase the probability of success in a problem solving situation".

Creativity becomes a conscious process through metaphoric activity of the Synectics Model. Metaphors establish a relationship of likeness, the comparison of one object or idea with another object or idea by using one in place of the other. Through these substitutions the creative process occurs, connecting the familiar with the unfamiliar or creating a new idea from familiar ideas. Three types of metaphors form the basis of Synectics exercise. They are:

1 Direct analogy

2 Personal analogy

3 Compressed conflicts

1. *Direct Analogy*: Direct analogy is a simple comparison of two objects or concepts. The comparison does not have to be identical in all respects.

2. *Personal Analogy*: The students have to empathize with the ideas or objects to be compared to make personal analogies. The identification may be with a person, animal or non living thing. A student may personally identify with molecules in action. He might think himself to be a part of the stream of dancing molecules and think of how he would feel being a molecule. In personal analogy one transports oneself into another object. This requires a loss of self.

Gordon identifies four levels of involvement in personal analogy.

i) *First-person description of facts*: The student just lists well-known facts about the object but does not view it in any new way or does not show any empathetic involvement. For example, in terms of a train, the students said, "I carry passengers, I run on rails".

ii) *First-person identification with emotion*: The student lists common emotions but does not present new sights. For example, "I feel proud to have the highest number of wheels".

iii) *Empathetic identification with a living thing*: The student identifies emotionally and kinesthetically with the subject of the analogy. For example, "I smile when people smile at me when I arrive at the station".

iv) *Empathetic identification with a non-living object*: The student sees himself in an organic object and tries to explore the problem or concept from a sympathetic point of view. This level requires the highest commitment. For example, "I feel sad that I have to run in the hot sun and rain" or "I feel helpless when I emit smoke and pollute the environment and cannot do anything to clean it".

These levels of personal analogy provide us with guidelines for how well conceptual distance has been established. According to Gordon the analogies are more useful, if the distance created is more. The greater the distance, the more the new ideas are created.

3. *Compressed conflicts*: It is generally a two word description of an object in which the words seem to be opposites or contradict each other. For example sympathetic revolutionary, nourishing flame and tiredly aggressive are compressed conflicts.

Stretching exercises:

Stretching exercises are given to provide students the experience with the three types of metaphoric activity. They are not related to any particular teaching-learning situation . They do not follow any sequence of phases. This is to teach students the process of metaphoric thinking before asking them to explore a concept or solve a problem. In stretching exercises students are simply asked to respond to ideas like

Direct analogies:

How is a vacuum cleaner like a monster?

How is your computer like a professor/ a servant?

How is a human brain like a library?

How is a book like a river?

How is an examination like a cricket match?

Personal analogies:

Be a ship: Describe yourself. How would you look like? What are you doing? What are the different situations you may come across and how do you feel in those situations?

Be a flower: Where are you? What are you doing? How would you feel when somebody admires you? How would you feel when somebody plucks you? What are your three wishes?

Compressed conflicts:

How is a man hot and cool?

How is your bike a friend and an enemy?

Some of responses given by students during stretching exercises for personal and direct analogy are given in appendix C (IV-a) and C (IV-b) respectively.

Analogies and learning

Learning is meaningful when an idea fits within the

conceptual framework or the mental scheme of the learners. An analogy provides a bridge between an unfamiliar concept and the knowledge the students possess. There can be situations where actual performing of an experiment is either not possible or demands a lot of time to reach at the final result. For ex: Looking into an atom or decay of a radioactive nucleus is not an easy thing to be perceived in a classroom. Abstract concepts such as structure of nucleus, motion of a body on a frictionless surface, wave nature of light, temperature, sound propagation and many other concepts cannot be easily taught and understood, unless suitable analogies are used.

Analogies are not merely illustrative or descriptive. In education, analogical reasoning is considered to be a process of identifying similarities between two concepts. It has two basic components. According to Glynn, the familiar concept is called an analog and the unfamiliar science concept is called target. For every concept or target the analog has to be appropriately selected, if possible from the students' world. Features of this analog must have many similarities with the target and should help in bringing about conceptual changes. However, the features of the analog, which are unlike the target if not suitably pointed out, may lead to impaired learning.

In order to have a systematic approach to using analogies, Glynn suggested a six-point strategy in "teaching with analogies". The six points are:

i) Introduce the target concept to be learned.

ii) Cue the students' memory of the analogous situation.

iii) Identify the relevant features of the target concept and the analog.

iv) Map out the similarities between the target concept and the analog.

v) Indicate where the analogy breaks down.

vi) Draw conclusions about the target concept.

Use of analogical reasoning enhances students' learning through constructivistic path. Students attempt to integrate new ideas with the preconceptions or alternative frameworks. The teacher should recognize that the students have their own perception of natural or technological world around them. This aspect should be taken as a gift rather than a hurdle to new learning.

Choice of analogy is of prime importance. It becomes a determining factor for bringing about conceptual changes. For example, radioactive decay could be explained using coins, dices or liquid coming out of the nozzle of a burette. The relationship between objects or terms provide the basis for analogical mapping. For example, when an electron moving around a nucleus is compared to the solar system, in which planets revolve around the sun, the idea that both solar system and atom involve particles revolving around a central particle could be grasped by the mind easily. At the same time, it could be seen that in both these cases gravitational force or attraction is working.

When an analogy is constructed, similarities come to mind immediately and can be easily inferred. It is not only similarities that are to be dealt with but the limitations i.e. where any particular analogy breaks down also require suitable interpretations after being identified. Reasoning with analogies facilitates individuals in growth of knowledge by enabling them to generate new inferences. Use of analogical reasoning has an important cognitive role to play in bringing about conceptual changes amongst the students.

Shapiro(1985) has discussed the use of analogy in the learning process that is of importance: analogies may make new information more concrete and easier to imagine. This is also highlighted by several other authors(Black, 1976; Davidson, 1976; Paivio, 1983). According to 'constructivistic view' learning is not intake of 'nuggets of truth' (Kelly 1955), but a process of actively employing the already familiar to understand the unfamiliar. Learning, therefore, fundamentally has to do with constructing similarities between the new and the already known.

More 'traditional' views of learning (e.g., Gagne, 1970) also emphasize, of course, the necessity of relating the unfamiliar to the familiar. Analogies are of pivotal importance in conceptual change learning in that they may help to restructure existing memory and to prepare it for new information (Geutner, 1983; Shapiro, 1985). Employing an analogy does not merely help or facilitate learning in a new domain, it also opens up new perspectives for viewing and, hence, restructuring the analog. Using an analogy is, therefore, essentially a "two way" process involving developing both analog and target (Bauer and Richter, 1986; Steiner, 1988).

Syntax of Synectics Model of teaching

There are two strategies or models of teaching based on Synectics procedure. One of these 'creating something new' is designed to make the familiar strange. This helps the students to see old problems, ideas or products in a new more creative light. The other strategy 'making the strange familiar' is designed to make new, unfamiliar ideas more meaningful. Creating something new is referred to as strategy one and making the strange familiar is referred to as strategy two.

The syntax of strategy one appears in Table 1.1 and that of strategy two appears in Table 1.2.

Table 1.1 Syntax for (Creating Something New) Making Familiar Strange, Strategy One.

PHASE ONE	PHASE TWO
DESCRIPTION OF PRESENT CONDITION	DIRECT ANALOGY
Teacher has students describe situation or situations as they see it now.	Students suggest direct analogies, select one and explore(describe) it further.
PHASE THREE	**PHASE FOUR**
PERSONAL ANALOGY	COMPRESSED CONFLICT
Students "become" the analogy they selected in phase two	Students take their descriptions from phase two and three, suggest several compressed conflicts, and choose one.
PHASE FIVE	**PHASE SIX**
DIRECT ANALOGY	RE-EXAMINATION OF THE ORIGINAL TASK
Students generate and select another direct analogy, based on the compressed conflict	Teacher has students move back to original task or problem and use the last analogy and the entire Synectics experience.

Table 1.2 : Syntax for Making the Strange Familiar, Strategy Two

PHASE ONE	PHASE TWO
SUBSTANTIVE INPUT	DIRECT ANALOGY
Teacher provides information on new topic.	Teacher suggests direct analogy and asks students to describe the analogy
PHASE THREE	**PHASE FOUR**
PERSONAL ANALOGY	COMPARING ANALOGIES
Teacher has students "become" the direct analogy	Students identify and explain the points of similarity between the new material and the direct analogy.
PHASE FIVE	**PHASE SIX**
EXPLAINING DIFFERENCES	EXPLORATION
Students explain where the analogy does not fit	Students re-explore the original topic on its own terms.

PHASE SEVEN

GENERATING ANALOGY

Students provide their own direct analogy and explore the similarities and differences.

The two strategies are more or less, similar up to phase three. In phase four, strategy one, creating something new-compressed conflict has been introduced, while in strategy two, making strange familiar- compressed conflict has been omitted. Here students use only direct and personal analogy. The major difference between the two strategies lies in the use of analogy. In strategy one, students move through a series of analogies without logical constraints; conceptual distance is increased, and imagination is free to wander. In strategy two, students try to connect two ideas and try to identify the connections as they move through the analogies. The strategy the teacher selects depends on whether he or she is trying to help the students create something new or to explore the familiar.

Social system: The model is moderately structured. The students have freedom for open-ended discussions as they engage in metaphorical problem solving. Norms of co-operation, "play of fancy", and intellectual and emotional equality are essential.

Principles of reaction: The teacher has to induce psychological states which is essential to generate creative response. The teacher herself should be a model. The teacher should accept and encourage the student to indulge in irrelevance, fantasy, symbolism, the non-rational and other devices necessary. The teacher should accept all student responses to ensure that students do not feel any external judgments on their creative expression. Far-fetched analogies should be accepted so that students develop fresh perspectives on problems or concepts. Students should be guarded against pre-mature analysis in strategy two.

Support system: A synectics group needs a teacher competent in synectics procedures. The class requires its own work space and an environment in which creativity is prized and utilized. A typical classroom is sufficient. But a classroom-sized group is too large for synectics activities, and smaller groups have to be created.

Instructional and Nurturant Effects:

The Synectics Model contains strong elements of both instructional and nurturant values as shown in figure 1.1.

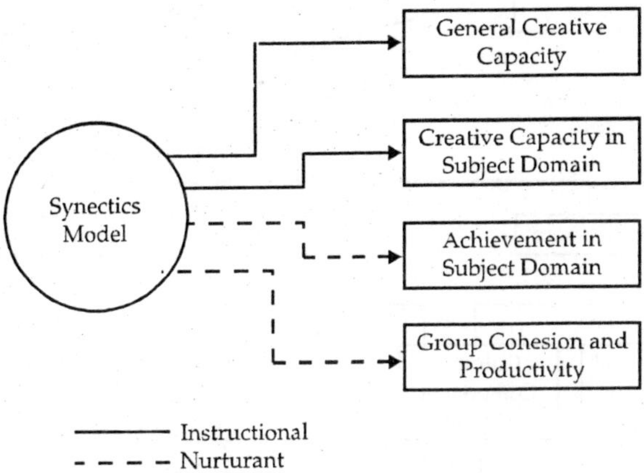

Fig 1.1 Instructional and nurturant effects : Synectics Model.

The method of Synectics has been explicitly designed to improve the creativity of individuals and groups. However, the implicit learning from this model is equally vivid. Participation in a Synectics group invariably creates a unique shared experience that fosters interpersonal understanding and a sense of community. Each thought, no matter how prosaic, is valued for its potential catalytic effect on one's own thoughts. The playfulness of Synectics activities encourages even the most timid participant.

General creative capacity and creative capacity in subject domain are the instructional effects of Synectics model of teaching. This creative capacity has to be developed by adopting Synectics model through teaching of a subject. Since creativity and problem solving ability are implicit in science teaching and learning, application of Synectics model of teaching to develop creativity and problem solving ability throu gh science would be a judicious and imperative task.

Figure 1.2 shows the philosophical, sociological and psychological components involved in welding together the institutions of science and education through curriculum and instruction.

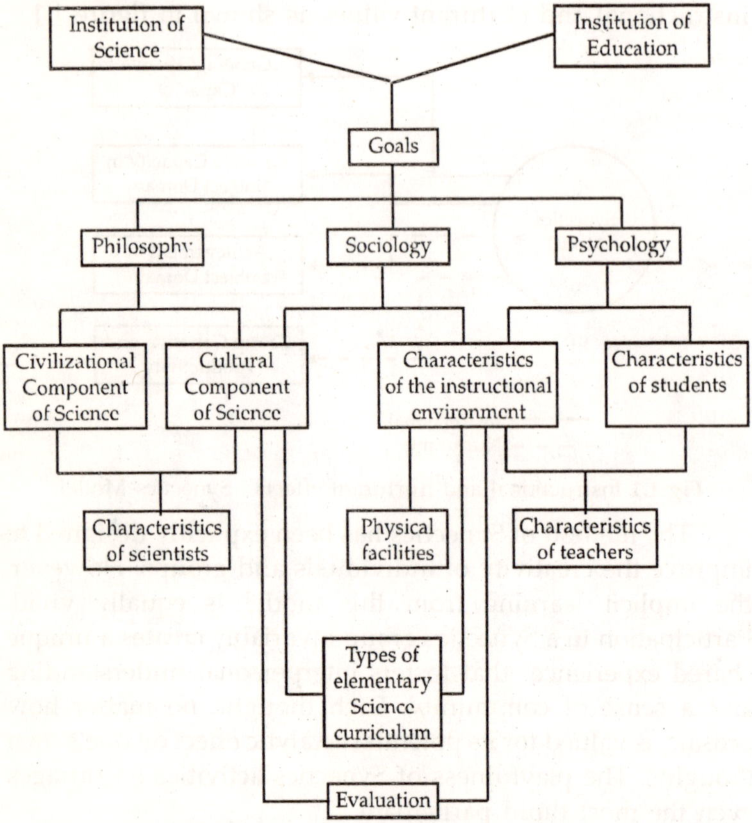

Fig. 1.2 : Philosophical, sociological and psychological components involved in welding together the institutions of science and education through curriculum and instruction.

Just as the sciences grow and change our time, so do the programs of education that adults think will best ensure the future of the next generation. Guided by the perspectives of a given era, curriculum writers choose content and problems most likely to equip the next generation approximately. But of course, they cannot know the future in all its detail, so each program is a kind of guess. Each year in which children take part in the educational enterprise, society in the person of their teachers and parents, guides them according to the knowledge it has at the time. Whether they receive the mental and spiritual nourishment of the sort that will help remains to be seen. Education of the young is a kind of experiment in which the results are not all realized at one particular time. Creative capacity, problem solving ability and scientific outlook are the basis for wholistic science. Thus strengthening of science teaching at primary and secondary levels becomes an urgent need. Before going into science teaching, we need to know the specific meaning of 'science'.

1.2 Meaning of Science

It is indisputable that today science is the byword and that the scientific aspect of things is emphasized wherever one goes. Science is the central enterprise of the societies populating the planet earth. Still virtually anywhere in the world that we might stop to inquire, science means almost nothing to the average person. Yet its impact on all of us is growing. Science is known to many people because of its applications and not its theories.

Our environment to a great degree is influenced by science. The clothing we wear, the houses we build and live in, the agricultural methods which produce our food, our automobiles, our electrical appliances used are all based upon scientific information. Our environment would be entirely changed if it were not for our continual exposure to the results of the application of scientific principles. Industry would still be an infant if it were not for science. Without science most of our luxuries and comforts would be unknown. It has helped in the reduction of pain and human suffering which accompany diseases and injuries of the human mechanism. It has shrinked the world and made it more accessible. It has controlled health, transportation and power. It is the technological innovations derived from science that determine the character of a nation.

In terms of the policy, the Government of India adopted in 1968, "it is an inherent obligation of a great country like India, with its tradition of scholarship and original thinking and its great cultural heritage, to participate fully in the march of science, which is probably making greatest enterprise today".

The term science or scientia is etymologically synonymous with knowledge. Science is classified knowledge gained from a systematic study of behavior of nature. It is comparatively easier to experience science than define it.

Science Manpower Project defines, "Science is a cumulative and endless series of empirical observations which result in the formation of concepts and theories, with both concepts and theories being subject to modification in the light of further empirical observations. Science is both a body of knowledge and the process of acquiring it".

The Columbia Encyclopedia (1963) defines science as an accumulated and systematized learning , in general usage restricted to natural phenomenon. It also states that the progress of science is marked not only by an accumulation of facts, but by the emergence of scientific method and scientific attitude.

According to Gagne (1965), 'Science is what the scientist does. It is a process by which we increase and refine understanding of ourselves and of the universe through continuous observation, experimentation, application and verification'.

From these definitions it is evident that science is a body of knowledge acquired through scientific method of inquiry. This indicates that science is both a product and a process.

'Accumulation of Knowledge', forms the product side of science. Science is being taught in our schools as a body of established facts obtained by individuals using infallible methods. Our present classroom practices emphasize on this product side of science rather than the method of acquiring this knowledge which is the scientific method which forms the process side of science. Observation, classification, making inferences, formulating and testing hypotheses, and conducting of experiments of natural phenomena are processes which form the process of science.

In an attempt to define processes in science the American Association for Advancement of Science(AAAS) asked scientists to reveal, what they actually do. This inquiry led to the following identifications.

a) Observation

b) Classification

c) Number relations

d) Measurement

e) Space/time relations

f) Communication

g) Prediction

h) Inference

i) Making operational definitions

j) Formulating hypotheses

k) Interpreting data

l) Identifying and controlling variables

m) Experimenting.

In Karl Pearson's Scheme, the following eight were the major steps of scientific method.

a) Sensing the problem including its definition, scope and analysis.

b) Experimentation

c) Collection of data, interpretation of data, selecting and examining the most fruitful hypothesis and arriving at a tentative solution.

d) Establishment of the law

e) Centralization of the law (theory)

f) Application of the law to new situation.

g) Predictability

h) Idealization and abstraction.

In brief the scientific method consists of i) making an accurate survey of the problem ii) setting up the method of attacking the problem iii) collecting data regarding the problem and iv) drawing conclusions from the data which have been collected. By looking at these steps, the terms scientific method and problem solving method could be synonymously used. It could be said that scientific method is the method or steps followed to solve problems.

The scientific method has expanded into almost every area of human activity. It has been largely responsible for the progress achieved in the fields of medicine, industry, business, psychology and education. It has been made the standard mode of application to all the social and physical problems which are encountered by thinking people.

1.3 History of Science Teaching

Undoubtedly India heralded the movement in the field of mathematics, medicine, astronomy etc. The concept of atom and science is mentioned in the Upanishads and the Vedas. Surgery existed though in a crude form. But this knowledge was confined only to limited number of individuals. Due to lack of written material everything vanished.

Educational systems of Greeks and Romans had little place for science. Teaching of science was in its juvenile stage during Pluto and Aristotle. Comenius was the first man who unfurled the flag of teaching science in secondary schools(1522 - 1670). Rousseau(1712 - 1778), Pestalozzi(1746 - 1827) and Froebel(1782 - 1852) recognized the use of natural objects. They were probably turning to their environments.

Science in modern sense is hardly three centuries old. It is difficult to say exactly when science teaching in schools began. Progress in the acceptance of science as a subject worthy of place in the educational program was very slow. A review of the historical development of science teaching reveals several forces which effectively retarded the development of scientific study and teaching. Among these were i) religious influences and ii) college entrance requirements.

(i) *Religious influences*: The atmosphere of the early colonial days was a strongly religious one. Scientific information which did not conform to the religious beliefs were deliberately withheld by the teachers and writers. Later the authors used facts from biological sciences which tended to prove the creator to be wise and benevolent and to strengthen the student's belief in the supernatural ordering of natural events.

(ii) *College entrance requirements*: One of the major purpose of the early college was to prepare young men for the ministry, and the requirements for admission to the institutions of higher learning were limited to proficiency in Latin and Greek. Science was not accepted for college entrance until 1872 when Harvard added physics to the approved list of preparatory subjects. This was rapidly followed by other institutions and the honor extended to other science subjects. Because of the lack of standardization in the secondary schools, the college proceeded to dictate in detail the nature of science instruction which would be accepted by them. During this time laboratory instruction became very popular and the paramount objective of science teaching was to develop the faculties of reasoning, observation, concentration, sensory training and the like.

General science is a relative late-comer into the secondary school curriculum. It had its beginning between 1910 and 1915. By 1930, a majority of the schools were teaching general science.

Although the Physical Science Study Committee (PSSC) was organized prior to the launching of Sputnik to improve the physical science instruction in United States senior high schools, this event greatly influenced the activity of this committee in developing course materials and equally affected the many new science programs which were developed shortly thereafter: the BSCS(Biological Science Curriculum Study) with its several versions, CHEMS (Chemical Education Material Study), CBA (Chemical Bond Approach) Project, ESCP(Earth Science Curriculum Project), the SCIP(Science Curriculum Improvement Project). The Harvard Physics Project, the Princeton Project in science for the junior high school and others belong to the latter category.

Science teaching in India is several decades old and of course, it started on a very slow foot. The pattern of education was influenced by what happened in England. The reviews issued by the Government of India in the year 1877 - 92 gave insight into the sorry state of science teaching. The Report of the Secondary Education Commission (1953), recommended the teaching of General Science as compulsory subject in the high and higher secondary schools. All India seminar on

Teaching of Science(1956) touched almost all the aspects concerning the teaching of science in schools viz., syllabus, equipment and apparatus method of examination, teaching aids and other allied topics like Text Books, Science Clubs, Museum etc. It suggested an unique and uniform system of science teaching for the entire country, suited to its needs and resources.

UNESCO Planning Mission(1963-1964) gave their recommendations in different aspects of science education and suggested ways to improve it. As a follow-up programme of this report, the Department of Science Education in the National Council, took up the pilot projects of preparing new curriculum, text books, teacher's guides etc. A conference of science education was convened from 21st and 23rd April, 1966 under the chairmanship of Dr. Kothari, to plan an effective programme for the development of the total curriculum of science education for different stages. Indian, Russian, American and UNESCO experts in science education participated in the conference.

Indian Education Commission(1964 - 66) pointed out that our science education is in bad shape and it becomes worse if we fail to reckon with the explosion of knowledge. It recommended upgrading school curricula by research in curriculum development, the revision of text books and teaching learning material.

1.4 Present Status of Science Teaching

In spite of all the institutions and recommendations of various committees the present status of science teaching is not satisfactory. The NCERT(1961) has given a report on the present system of science education. It is reported that the knowledge which the students have is bookish. Laboratories are just an eyewash in some schools and in others they do not exist. Equipments in the laboratory are not sufficient. Science is not related to daily life of students and the practical applications of it. Teachers still continue with lecture methods. Methods of teaching are old and worn out. Learning by doing is still a slogan packed in the books. Individual attention is not paid. Spirit of investigating individually is not at all encouraged.

The present teaching methods do not cater to the needs of all categories of children and do not help in fulfillment of the aims and objectives of science. Development of the spirit of inquiry, ability to solve problems and creativity in students which are the main aims of science teaching are completely neglected in present day science teaching.

1.4.1 Aims and Objectives of Teaching Science

Science teaching in schools has several functions to perform. It must give the student a systematic training in careful observation, in experiment and in the estimation of the relative value of results. It must provide a knowledge of the material world and of the forces of nature and must lay a sound foundation for more advanced work. Science requires exact and accurate observations, care and thoroughness of techniques, the logical interpretation of data and the intelligent estimation of the reliability of results.

A philosophy of science teaching is made up of the aims and objectives of teaching in general and of science teaching in particular. The objectives of science teaching may be classified into categories which are different in scope. The general aims of education which seem to be functional are, "Training for efficient participation in a Democratic Society", "Training for citizenship", "Individual development", "Social Efficiency", or the like.

The major aims of teaching science are:

- to give students broad genuine appreciation of what development of science means to modern, social, industrial and national life.

- to satisfy natural interest in things and forces of nature with which men are surrounded.
- to provide opportunity for students to become acquainted with application of science for the purpose of educational and vocational guidance and possibility of furnishing a beginning of vocational training.
- to develop broad concepts and natural laws to the end that science and reality may function in place of superstitions and uncertainty in explaining natural phenomenon.
- to contribute such specific ideals, habits and concepts of accuracy, achievement, persistence, open mindedness, honesty etc.
- to develop system, order to the end that they shall function in ordinary affairs of life.
- to stimulate spirit of investigation and invention on the part of the student.
- to provide opportunities for acquaintance with application of science in public utility in order that student may fulfill the duties of citizenship.
- to provide opportunities for acquaintance with such applications of science which contribute to maintenance of health of individual and community.

Various functional objectives are stated based on these aims. Main objectives of science teaching for entire programme of science teaching in secondary schools are as given below.

1. Knowledge

This objective implies the student to acquire the knowledge of

- fundamental principles and concepts useful in daily life

- a body of facts to understand the scientific literature
- interrelationship and interdependence of different branches of science
- knowledge of plants, animals- their interdependence
- knowledge of natural phenomenon
- knowledge of origin of evolution of plants and animals, origin of earth, moon and other planets and satellites
- knowledge of general rules of health and human body

The student should be able to apply this knowledge in his daily life.

2. Skills

The student should acquire skill in experimentation, construction, observation, drawing and problem solving.

3. Abilities

The teaching of science should also aim at developing certain abilities in the students such as ability to sense a problem, organize and interpret, analyze, generalize, predict from given data, locate reliable and necessary information from appropriate source, improvize and manipulate instruments using his acquired knowledge, and to discuss, agree and express using scientific terminology.

4. Attitudes

Scientific attitudes are the most important outcomes of science teaching.

A man with scientific attitude

- is critical in observation and thought
- is open minded

- respects other's point of view and is ready to change his decision on presentation of new and convincing evidence.
- is curious to know more about things around him, wants to know 'why', 'what' and 'hows' of the things he observes
- is objective in his approach to problems
- does not believe in superstition and false beliefs
- suspends judgements until suitable support is obtained
- believes in cause and effect relationship
- is truthful in his observation and draws conclusions based on accurate facts
- is unbiased and impartial in his judgement
- adopts a planned procedure in solving a problem
- believes that truth never changes, but his ideas of what is true may change as he gains better understanding of that truth
- accepts no conclusion as final or ultimate
- seeks to adopt various techniques and procedure to solve the problem
- selects the most recent, authoritative and accurate evidence related to the problem
- seeks the facts and avoids exaggeration

5. Interests

Children should feel alive in the environment they live in. There are multifarious desires and fun sense among the children that are to be rationalized and channelized through scientific activities.

6. Appreciations

The basic aim here is to give students a real feel and admiration of science. A few area for developing scientific appreciations. The problem of spare time is easily solved through the teaching of science by making students, conscious of the scientific activities like preparing articles of daily use, improvisation, preparing charts and models, collecting seeds, leaves, minerals etc. These activities can become useful and productive afterwards when perfection is achieved.

7. Forming basis for vocational career

The syllabus of science prepares students for certain vocations such as those of doctors, engineers, research scholars, agricultural experts etc. Thus it is also an important aim of science teaching to prepare the students for better living.

8. Training for reflective thinking (scientific method)

It means to prepare the students in such a way that they attack every problem with planned procedure and to enable them to apply it in every new situation. It involves the following steps:-

- Sensing problem- That the problem exists.
- Defining problem - The problem should be defined and clarified.
- Analyzing the problem- The problem should be analyzed in steps.
- Collecting data- The facts relevant to the problem concerned should be accumulated.
- Interpreting problem - The data collected are arranged in such a way as to reach the generalizations, tracing out the basic principles involved.

- Selecting most likely results - superfluous data irrelevant to the problem is rejected through discussions.
- Drawing conclusions and induction and application to other situation similar to it.

1.4.2 Objectives of Teaching Science as suggested in various Reports

All India Seminar on Teaching of Science Taradevi Report(1956) suggested the following aims of science teaching in secondary schools.

- To familiarize the pupil with the world in which he lives and to make him understand the impact of science on society so as to enable him to adjust himself to his environment.
- To acquaint him with the 'Scientific Method' and to enable him to develop the scientific attitude.
- To give the pupil a historical perspective, so that he may understand the evolution of the scientific development.

Ishwarbhai Patel Committee(1977) stated the objectives of secondary education as given below:

- Acquisition of the skills and habits of self-learning;
- Acquisition of a broad-based general education consisting of science, mathematics, social sciences, languages and socially useful productive labor;
- Developing Aesthetic Appreciation and Creativity through participation in artistic activities.

1.5 Creativity and Science

"Whether they serve in governments or factories, hospitals or universities, villages or business houses, creative leaders are sorely needed by every society. Particularly in a developing country, the economic innovator - a man willing to introduce new techniques, bear the risks of failure, and assume responsibility for change - must take the lead. Clearly, creative men are urgently needed on every strata of society .... traditional societies must seek out, train and tangibly aid their potential innovators".

-McCord (1965)

1.5.1 Meaning of Creativity

Creativity makes our lives happy and comfortable. An ordinary individual who is engaged in a simple occupation, if creative can through creativity add new quality and beauty to his products. The impact of creativity is to make an activity or object better, richer, more productive and fruitful. Creativity is the most important inborn instinct of a child. Children can be creative and can experience the process of creativity. This brings us to the question as to what is creativity. The definitions of the term creativity range in scope and complexity from simple problem-solving to the actualization of self. A few definitions relevant from the point of view of the present study are discussed here.

The *New Encyclopedia Britannica* defines creativity as "the ability to make or otherwise bring into existence something new, whether a new solution to a problem, a new method or device or new artistic object of form". This is the most obvious approach to the subject, since the products being public and readily available are more easily assessed.

Torrance(1969) defines creative thinking as "the process of sensing gaps or disturbing, missing elements, forming ideas or hypotheses, possibly modifying and re-testing hypotheses and finally communicating the results".

This definition gives more importance to the process of thinking than the product of it, while the earlier one emphasized the product.

James (1979) quotes the definition of creativity given by Einstein which is a combination of the two approaches. It reads as "Creativity is a specific form of problem - solving behavior, characterized by originality; which means production of new ideas".

Mackinnon (1968) discusses four approaches to understanding creativity

- the creative product
- the creative process
- the creative person and
- the creative situation (press).

These are popularly known as product, process, person and press approaches.

1.5.2 Characteristic Traits of Creative Students

Who is creative? How does one recognize creative people? Would a study of phrenology or physiognomy help in this identification? While there may be internal creativity, overt acts are necessary to communicate it to others. Creativity involves "originality" and a person who exhibits unique and original performances over a period of time can be called a 'creative person'. Creative persons usually

- have a healthy appetite towards and a dedication to work and prefer variety in the work.
- are persistent in the pursuit of problems.
- have an abundant amount of energy and apply it in a disciplined manner.
- enjoy manipulating objects as well as ideas.
- have a strong ego.

- feed on recognition.
- enjoy thinking and accept challenges.
- exhibit an impatience to get on with the work at hand.
- resist an over abundance of supervision.
- are not prone to worry about inconsistencies, but look for them.
- are not anxious to conclude matters prematurely but prefer to investigate various skepticisms before assigning finality to problems.
- are critical of current solutions to problems.
- are sensitive to change and have a high irritability factor to what does not seem right to them.
- enjoy shuffling and expanding ideas.
- can entertain dichotomous consideration in the flow of thoughts as directed toward the solution of problems.
- are curious and wonder about themselves and how and 'why' of things.
- are willing to take a change and risk security by extending their thinking beyond conventional boundaries.

E.P. Torrance summarized the personality traits of highly creative persons. His list included the following:

- strong affection.
- always baffled by something.
- attracted to mysterious.
- attempts difficult jobs(sometimes too difficult).
- bashful outwardly.

- constructive in criticism.
- courageous.
- deep and conscientious convictions.
- defies conventions of courtesy.
- defies convention of health.
- desires to excel.
- determination.
- differentiated value -hierarchy.
- discontented.
- receptive to ideas of others.
- regresses occasionally.
- reserved.
- resolute.
- self-starter.
- sense of destiny.
- shuns power.
- sincere.

From the above list it is clear that everybody possess the creative potential in varying degrees and nobody has all the above characteristics to the same degree. Creativity occurs at almost all ages in all fields of human endeavor. A creative artist or musician produces new, original, unique paintings or music; a creative engineer produces new, original, unique ideas or constructs. And so teachers dubbed "creative" produce new, original, unique learning situations where in students can create new, original, unique solutions to problems and discover new patterns, new ideas or new products.

Creativity can be developed and its development depends upon the environment into which it is introduced and circumstances that condition it.

The personality test results of highly creative people provide some important traits, even though there may be contrary results in some experiments (Barron, 1955; Mackinnon, 1962; Roe, 1952). A general picture of the productively creative person would be like this:

- He is dominant, possessed of those qualities and attributes which underlie and lead to achievement of personal status, poised, spontaneous, self-confident in social interaction, although not of an especially sociable-temperament, intelligent, outspoken, sharp-witted, demanding, aggressive and self-centered, persuasive and verbally fluent and relatively uninhibited in expressing his worries and complaints.
- He is comparatively free from conventional restraints and inhibitions, not pre-occupied with the impression he makes on others and thus, he is capable of great independence and autonomy.
- He is not inclined to strive for achievement in settings where conforming behavior is expected or required. In efficiency and steadiness of intellectual efforts, however, he does not differ from his fellow workers. Finally, he is definitely more psychologically minded, more flexible, and possessed of more feminity of interests than less creative persons.

Some of the traits mentioned above seem to be manifested functionally in quite opposite directions in individual personalities, but the general picture however, signify the creative persons. Some of these personality traits may be found in ordinary persons, but they do not become highly creative, because they have to be specialized in some field and apply the creative process to produce a creative product.

1.5.3 Creativity and Science Teaching

Education commission(1964 - 66) opines

"The aim of education can no longer be the mere imparting of knowledge or preparation of a finished product, but it is the training of character to fit the students to participate creatively as citizens in the emerging democratic order. Therefore, a function of the school is to provide opportunities for creative growth as democracy matures and flourishes on the creative efforts of its pupils, who later become the adults. But, what of it, in the schools of today?"

Creativity is certainly a word that is used rather loosely today, relative to teaching and learning. It is increasingly being heralded as the hallmark of all that is good and vital in the learning process. Creativity is recognized as a desired product of learning.

Creativity is a thinking process. Creative thinking differs from critical thinking in that it is concerned with new ideas as opposed to previous ideas or reflections on someone else's ideas. Creativity is the act of drawing on all past experiences and the act of selection from these to yield a construct of new pattern, new ideas or new products. The key word appears to be 'new': new to whom? Usually we are concerned with the newness being related to its contribution to society. However, if an elementary-school student generates a new idea - new to him - this would be temporarily sufficient. His contribution to society can come later. Some what like the expression; "Science is what scientists do", "creativity is what creative people do". Science is nothing but creative thinking and creative doing.

According to Indian Parliamentary and Scientific Committee(1964) "Science in our culture is a creative intellectual activity leading to unifying concepts of man's natural environment".

It is generally accepted that creativity is highly desirable and precious commodity and prized by teachers, scientists, engineers, industrialists, politicians, advertisers and others.

Despite research done in the past and currently in progress, little is known about those experiences and conditions that foster creativity. However it is generally accepted that creativity can be developed in students if in the learning process the teacher initiates creative situations to which students can react accordingly. Creativity teaching demands creative teachers.

James A. Smith states, "There are currently several barriers to creativity teaching which must be removed. Chief among these are: lack of intelligence, excessive conformity to pre-determined methods of teaching or teaching plans, over planning for classroom teaching, making the same plans for all children, the excessive use of stereotyped questions, the improper use of gimmicks, the overuse of text books as a teaching device, the inability on the part of the teachers and administrators to differentiate between research and the opinion of the experts, and the attitude and practices of the school administrator who does not recognize the value of unique performance among his personnel".

Smith further states, "Creativity as such, cannot be taught. It is not a subject or a skill which can be learned like history or demonstrated like baseball. It is an inborn, developmental quality, like love and can only be developed. Various aspects of creative thinking and doing can be modified through learning to the degree that all learning can be modified. But, because creativity is a quality already present in every individual, it needs to be coddled to help to develop. The uncreative children in our schools today are live testimony to the degree to which it can be killed off easily. Once it appears on the surface its reappearance can be assured by use of all those techniques which cause behavior to reappear. But it does not appear unless certain conditions are present which cause it to come forth. The problem, then seems to be to get it to reappear so the teacher can work with it, and by re-enforcement stimulate its reappearance, in other words set conditions for creativity".

The school should provide an environment that nurtures creativity. This environment should be a composite of conditions that allow creativity to flourish. These are:

- an intellectual atmosphere
- the necessary physical environment
- a climate for creative expression
- adequate educational conditions.

The teacher and the school should provide not only the environment but also resources for the development of varied and related experiences. The elements of convergent and divergent thinking should be continuously stressed and applied to the solution of problems throughout the entire curriculum.

Creative teachers need to develop specific intellectual skills like deductive thinking, the ability to see relationships and the ability to analytically observe the components and inherent properties of objects within a system.

Science is a creative venture. Creativity is as vital at the frontier of science as it is within the interior. Science grows when new facts are added to old and when new concepts and theories are formulated. Science is thinking curiously and deriving new ideas from this creativity. Everyday more opportunities should be provided for children to think creatively, and to meet this need in part, it is recommended that children be provided with numerous Situational Science Experiences(SSE). SSEs are brief situations conjured up by the teacher or students to provide the class with short-term daily problems that provide exercise in creative thinking. Involvement in SSEs is often regulated primarily to "thinking" one's way through a particular situation. Conditions for creative development may be greatly enhanced by improving the physical aspects of the classroom environment.

Through the study of science, pupils learn that careful collection of data is often done through the use of instruments, and realize that through the refinements of instruments our scientific knowledge has grown. It is important to stress the possibilities for creativeness inherent in the use of instruments to make discoveries. Making and using science equipment is challenging to the imagination, resourcefulness, and creativeness of children.

The development of productive thinking and creativity among various groups of pupils at various ages right throughout the school is a major educational problem in the area of science education and teaching which has not been yet tackled satisfactorily in our country. This is because our educational system is still dominated by examination.

Science is natural for creativity. Science teaching and creativity should go hand in hand. The scientist is one of the most creative persons in our society- frontiers in science are constantly being advanced by his creations. The qualities or characteristics of scientists are in many ways analogous to those traits associated with creative individual.

Creative thinking is problem solving and more. Problems, experiments and opportunities for children wherein they can use their imagination, originality and curiosity will undoubtedly foster creativity.

1.6 Problem Solving and Science

Life is nothing but a series of problems. Experience in dealing with problems will help the individual in cultivating strategies which may prove to be of great value at crucial moments of life. Science concerns itself with the solution of many problems. What is a problem?! A 'problem' usually means a task that can be defined external to the individual such as a maze, puzzle, anagram, mathematical problem, or other task in which an observable or openly stated answer is provided.

According to Davis(1973): "A problem is a stimulus for which an organism doesn't have a ready response".

A problem is a situation, quantitative or otherwise that confronts an individual or group, that requires resolution, and for which the individual sees no apparent or obvious means or path to obtaining the solution. As people develop scientifically, what are problems initially are reduced to routine exercises. A problem must satisfy three criteria viz., acceptance, blockage and exploration.

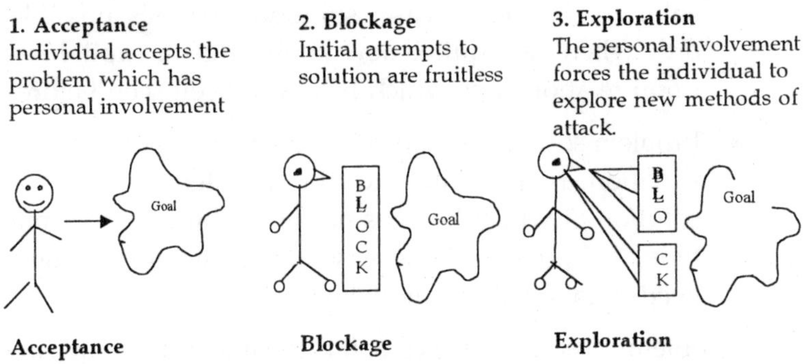

Fig. 1.3 Criteria of a Problem

A problem will no longer be a problem once it can easily be solved by algorithms that have been previously learned. What is a problem for someone may not be a problem for another who has more experience in the concerned field.

1.6.1 Problem Solving

This is the cry of the hour. Terms like concept formation, critical thinking, creative thinking, reasoning, insight and learning are a part of definitions of problem solving. Deliberately avoiding the use of these terms the following three definitions of problem solving are considered.

- Problem solving may be defined as a planned attack upon a difficulty or perplexity for the purpose of finding a solution. There is, then, recourse to reflective thinking which is a process of careful conscious consideration of facts, beliefs or other elements of mental experience for the purpose of arriving at rational conclusions relevant to some problem or perplexity.
- Problem-solving takes place when a problem-solver accepts to solve it as well as when his previous knowledge or patterns or behavior are insufficient or inappropriate to enable him to provide an acceptable solution. In such a case, solution becomes possible only when he acquires new knowledge or capitalizes upon relationships which have not been seen before.
- Problem solving takes place as soon as a task-oriented situation is presented to the problem-solver, the solution of which he does not know but, at the same time, he possesses the essential basic information needed to solve the problem.

Problem solving is a process. It is the means by which an individual uses previously acquired knowledge, skills and understanding to satisfy the demands of an unfamiliar situation. The student must synthesize what he has learnt and apply it to the new and different situation. Problem solving skills should be considered as a distinct body of knowledge and should be taught as such.

The knowledge of science can be divided into several parts, two of which are i) information and facts (ii) the ability to use information and facts. This ability to use information and facts is an essential part of the problem solving process.

A key factor in problem solving is the application of past experience or knowledge to arrive at a solution not previously known to the person at least in the particular situation presented. The fact that past experience supplies the requisite information or skills for solution distinguishes problem solving from learning.

1.6.2 Stages of Problem Solving

Several investigators have written about the stages of problem solving. One of the earliest was John Dewey(1910). The five stages given by him are:

- A felt difficulty;
- Its location and definition;
- Suggestion of possible solution;
- Development of reasoning of the bearing of suggestion; and
- Further observation and experiment leading to its acceptance or rejection.

Holfman and co-workers(1951) analyzing the objectives of problem solving gave the following steps:

i) Sensing problem

ii) Defining the problem situation

iii) Studying the situation for all facts and clues bearing upon the problem

iv) Making the best tentative explanation or hypothesis

v) Testing hypothesis by experimental or other means

vi) Accepting tentatively or rejecting the hypothesis or testing other hypothesis

vii) Drawing conclusions using the hypothesis for generalization in terms of similar problem situation.

Bossing has discussed a few essentials of reflective thinking which an individual shows at the time when engaged in the act of problem solving viz.,

i) Ability to sense the problem and emergence of problem

ii) Defining the problem

iii) Collecting the relevant data

iv) Interpreting the data

v) Consideration of evidence leading to formation of conclusion

vi) Testing conclusions or verification of solution.

It has been pointed out by psychologists that it is not necessary that the mind may follow the orderly sequence given. A person may get an intuitive understanding of the problem and may start with a hypothesis. He may proceed to verify it. Thus the stages may be skipped or greatly condensed.

1.6.3 Thought Process involved in Problem Solving

Recent analyses of cognition as information processing throw new light on problem solving as cognitive activity. These analysis attempt to account for the human mind's ability, with a limited capacity for processing information, to solve complex problems that require planning and strategy. Studies of expert problem solvers and computer simulations of problem - solving processes show that the solution of a complex problem requires:

- a rich store of organized knowledge about the content domain,
- a set of procedures for representing and transforming the problem, and

- a control system to guide the selection of knowledge and procedures.

Successful problem solving requires an active stance: the pupil should attempt to transform an interactable problem, simplifying it or representing it some other way, rather than waiting passively for an inspiration. When pupils write different versions of problems, modify problems to yield different solutions, and construct original problem they learn to distinguish between a problem and the various ways it can be posed. The information-processing approach stresses that problem characteristics are major determinants of problem solving behavior(Goldin and McClintock,1979). Problems can be put into categories according to the information-processing they require so that instruction can be concentrated on the processes needed to solve them. The topic of "problem type", however, needs careful handling by teachers. Experiences in several countries show that a strong emphasis in science instruction on the identification of problem types leads to a narrow approach to problem solving. Pupils are more likely to be flexible in dealing with problems of an unfamiliar type if they have encountered problems that superficially appear to be of the same type but are not.

1.6.4 What makes a Good Problem Solver?

There are certain common characteristics exhibited by good problem solvers.

- A good problem solver has a desire to solve problem
- He is extremely perseverant. They go back and try new approaches again and again if a particular one leads to a dead end. They refuse to quit and are not easily discouraged when incorrect.
- A variety of methods of attack are usually at their disposal. They will ask themselves many "What if....", questions.

- They show an ability to skip some of the steps in the solution process. They make connections quickly, notice irrelevant detail and require very few examples to generalize. They often lack concern about neatness while developing their solution process.
- They are not afraid to guess. They make educated guesses at solutions and attempt to verify them.
- They know what questions to ask themselves and what to do with the answers they receive as they think through the problem.

1.6.5 Reasoning in Problem Solving

Man's life is an endless stream of problems, situations for which the individual has no ready-made formula or solution. Being unequipped with the proper solution, he requires to think and reason before he can solve the problem. Reasoning is the highest form of thinking that needs a well organized brain. The process of reasoning requires two conditions—first, that the person's mind should have completely formed concepts, and second, that he should be endowed with the power of reaching decisions. It is because the children lack these two facilities that they are not able to reason. In the process of reasoning, the individual reasons from the past known circumstances to the present or future unknown conditions on the basis of past experience. In this manner, reasoning helps to reach certain conclusions concerning the future without anything having been achieved in actual practice. Evidently such an application needs some imagination as an essential part.

The concept of Reasoning: It is the ability to perceive and utilize abstract relationship; to be able to put together past experience in the solution of new problems. The origin of the concept of 'reasoning' as a method to arrive at truth dates back to early Greek civilization. It had its roots in the work of Ionian philosophers who, instead of explaining away observed phenomenon with a 'word' or 'words'(hypostatization), insisted upon suggesting a 'hypothesis' about the phenomenon to arrive at truth. Subsequently, Socrates evolved his dialectical method. The Greek mathematicians including Pythagoras evolved the deductive method. Though Pythagoras is also credited with experimentation as a method to test the hypothesis, but his preference for deductive method led him to insist upon maintaining a hypothesis even though it was not substantiated by experimentation. It was left to Archimedes to reinstate the primacy of 'experimentation' for 'induction' and give some shape to 'scientific method' for reasoning, or to the inductive method. However, the work of Aristotle on formal logic, especially his method of syllogistic reasoning, did not let inductive method to flower till the end of dark-age and beginning of middle-age.

During the modern period, reasoning has been viewed in 'various ways'. Dewey(1899) has treated it almost as being synonymous with problem solving in which a person reasons out the solution of a problem in a systematic fashion, often making use of logical principles and relevant past experiences. He uses all his experiences relevant to the problems together to try-out various combinations until he arrives at the correct solution. Even those, who do not follow Dewey agree that reasoning does not occur until a problem or a difficulty is felt which cannot be solved by mere repetitions of earlier solutions, or by overt trial and error and for which there is no ready answer. To Burt 'reasoning' is an activity, the results of which are expressed by arguments made up of series of propositions or sentences logically connected(Burt 1949, pp 110 and 111). To Garrett, reasoning is thinking with a purpose or goal in which use is made of past experiences and in which organization and logical arrangement of responses is demanded(Garrett 1955, pp 414 - 418). To others, reasoning is a process of controlled thinking or association which starts with some problem of interest to the reasoner and directed towards its solution(Ellis 1965, p 219). To Stenberg, it is an attempt to combine elements of old information to form new information (Stenberg 1982, pp-235).

Be that as it may, two major forms of reasoning, induction and deduction have been a major concern among philosophers and psychologists during the last and early part of present century. The term 'induction' signifies from particular to general where as 'deduction' reasoning from general to particular, or more specifically from stated premises to a particular conclusion.

Reasoning is an essential part of problem solving which itself is regarded as a complex factor comprising induction, deduction and restrictive or general reasoning. Controversies on it are avoided by including it in problem solving.

1.6.6 Science Teaching and Problem Solving

Science is of great interest to children and is ever present. Science is concerned with explanations and resolution of problems. Its study provides a natural opportunity for children to grow in ability to solve problems. This growth in ability to solve problems is one of the primary contributions science can make.

Problem-solving in science involves the use of scientific habits and attitudes which include: careful observations, accurate interpretation of these observations, and skillful recording and communicating them. It includes the habit of withholding judgement, questioning sources of information, consulting many sources, and other familiar aspects of scientific attitude.

The cumulative aspect of science is that knowledge grows as it builds on other previous knowledge. In solving a science problem we do not start from the beginning instead we use what others have discovered and build on it. This is also true when pupils solve problems; it is also true when scientists solve problems.

Problem solving is an individual or group activity in which a question is posed, no route to the answer is indicated, the challenge of answering the question is accepted, and concepts and principles are used in seeking an answer. As a human endeavor, science has arisen out of the process of solving practical and intellectual problems. Despite the centrality of problem solving in science itself, however its role in the science curriculum is not very clearly established. Science educators agree that all children should be able to apply the science they have learned in school to the solution of problems they will face, but there is little agreement as to whether the science teacher can, or should attempt to, substantially improve children's ability to solve problems. Some teachers see their task as providing children with the knowledge and skills needed for subsequent problem solving and regard this task alone as sufficient to define the curriculum. Others believe that the curriculum should be organized around the solution of problems and that instruction should be aimed directly at improving problem solving ability.

Problem is a situation, where solution is to be found with the help of previously known information by applying scientific procedures.

Some recent curriculum programs have attempted to develop ways of leaving to the pupil all or part of the process of identifying a problematic situation, formulating a problem out of the situation, and then solving the problem. Increased attention in science instruction is being given to the use of "real problems": problems that are meaningful to the pupil and that require knowledge of the problem setting as well as knowledge of science.

An increasingly popular view is that the teacher should

provide instruction in problem-solving techniques and strategies but opinion differ as to the nature and extent of this instruction. Instead of teaching pupils to follow a fixed sequence of steps, some teachers have attempted to provide them with heuristic advice (Polya 1981) that may help them analyze the problem and transform it into something they can solve. Pupils are not likely to learn to apply such advice unless they are given many opportunities to see it applied, practice its application and identify cues to help decide when it might be appropriate. Effective instruction in heuristic techniques and strategies is difficult and time consuming to accomplish in the science classroom. Some research indicates that children posses an impressive array of thinking strategies but that in many classrooms they are inhibited from applying them. A considerable improvement in problem-solving performance can occur when pupils responses are encouraged and accepted and the classroom atmosphere is made less threatening. This could easily be done through the Synectics model of teaching science.

To find room for problem solving activities in a crowded science curriculum, the teacher needs a serious commitment to the importance of problem solving. Teachers find collections of problem material invaluable, but they are unlikely to devote much attention to instruction in problem solving techniques and strategies if they themselves have not had the opportunity, as students, to solve challenging problems (Polya 1981) and to reflect on the role of problem solving in science.

1.7 Creativity and Problem Solving

Is problem solving different from creativity? The answer depends upon the nature of the problem. Finding solutions to problems whose solutions are not known or finding a novel solution which is superior to known solutions will certainly be an act of creativity.

In problem solving we are concerned with finding a

workable solution to a problem rather than with the generation of ideas alone. Although generation of ideas is essential to problem solving, the number of such ideas is not the criterion. Rather, one must evaluate the final choice.

Creativity is the development of new mental patterns. It is an emotional process and an irrational one too. Problem solving is rational and intellectual but by adding the irrational we increase the likelihood that we will generate fresh ideas.

The selection of the best or the most creative solution for a problem is open to question as it may be subjective when problems have many answers. Is there a relationship between the tendency to produce innovative solutions(creativity) and success in solving difficult problems (problem solving ability). Colgrove(1968) took up an experiment with the purpose of determining whether students superior in solving difficult problems having objectively correct solutions, also achieve solutions rated "creative" or superior for a problem with several possible answers. Four difficult objective type problems were used to measure problem solving ability and the CWP problem was used for the subjective measure. The case produces three types of solutions i.e. old, new and integrative solutions. Integrative solution was regarded as 'creative' and 'superior'. Students who reached the integrative solution solved significantly more of the objective problems, and an increasing trend for integrative solutions with increasing success on objective problems was evident. It was concluded that superior problem solvers also generate solutions that are rated as creative when several solutions to a given problem are possible.

Problem solving is only one aspect of creativity. Creativity is more comprehensive than problem solving. Creativity has many facts like imaginative writing, aesthetic value etc. besides problem solving, though problem solving does constitute an important aspect of creativity.

1.8 Need and Importance of the Study

National Policy of Education(1987) in its report points out in para 8.18 that "the development of well defined abilities and values such as spirit of inquiry, creativity, objectivity and the courage to question in the child will help in strengthening science education".

Science is the product of creative thinking by scientists over a period of time. Children tend to be naturally creative, but their creativity is dampened as a result of authoritarian system of education. In the conventional method of teaching science there is very little chance to discover and foster the creative potentials of children. The discovery and development of creative genius of our youth should be the prime importance of our education. Teachers and educators, therefore have a great responsibility to children and society to see this ability is manifested to the maximum of the individuals potential.

At present, teaching of science has become rather content oriented and is not in conformity with aims and objectives of teaching science. Learning of science has been diluted to mere acquisition of knowledge and information about scientific facts, principles, laws and theories. But the prime objective of teaching science in individualistic perspective is to impart the ability to use the scientific method of problem solving and the technique of observation and experimentation in handling problems of life. Special efforts are needed to develop creativity and problem solving ability among secondary school children through specially designed models and effective use of them in class-room teaching.

"Synectics Model" developed by William J.J. Gordon aims at developing creativity in children. One of its important effects as claimed is it also develops problem solving ability. There is a need to test its effectiveness in terms of developing creativity and problem solving ability in children. Hence the present study was undertaken.

In addition to the above, a review of related literature highlights the fact that Indian studies related to this model of teaching especially for science are far and few. Though there are some studies on this model, they are in the subject of languages and most of them have adopted strategy one, 'creating something new' and no study has adopted strategy two, 'making strange familiar'. The researcher has selected strategy two for teaching in the subject of science, which makes the study significant.

2

Review of Related Literature Building on the Past

An attempt has been made to review the related studies to know the trend of research in the area of models of teaching. Further, an analysis of studies related to the various variables considered in the present investigation was done.

The reviewed studies have been classified under seven headings:

2.1 Studies related to models of teaching in general.

2.2 Studies related to training strategy for using models of teaching.

2.3 Studies related to developing models for teaching.

2.4 Studies related to fostering creativity.

2.5 Studies related to inducing problem solving ability.

2.6 Studies related to role of analogies in learning.

2.7 Studies related to Synectics model of teaching.

2.8 Conclusions

2.1 Models of Teaching in General

Related to the vital area - Models of Teaching, the first study in India at M.Ed. level was conducted on Advance Organizer Model by Buddhisagar(1979) at Indore, while at

Ph.D. level the first study was completed by Chitriv(1983) at Nagpur. In the studies conducted so far various models have been used to train students, teachers and teacher educators.The Models of teaching usually adopted by the researchers are those developed by Bruce Joyce and Marsha Weil (1980).

Battacharya, Gopal Chandra(1985) compared the effectiveness of teaching geography through Concept Attainment Model(CAM) and Inductive Thinking Model in relation to institutional resources. 324 students of class VIII from 30 secondary schools were selected by quota sampling technique. The tools used were Test of General Mental Ability or Intelligence by M.C. Joshi, Test of Study Habits and Attitude by M.C. Joshi and Panday, Educational Institution Resource Status Index(EIRS) , SES Index and Achievement test by the Researcher. The findings of the study indicated that Inductive Thinking Model emerged as the best suitable model for all types of institutions. High EIRS institution groups showed better achievement irrespective of the models and concept types than the low EIRS ones. There was no observable combined interaction effect between EIRS, models of teaching, types of concepts taught and achievement.

Pandey, S.N.(1986) studied the effectiveness of Advance Organizer Model (AOM) and Inquiry Training Models(ITM) for teaching social studies to class VIII students. Two experimental groups formed AOM group and ITM group consisting of 29 and 28 students respectively. The control group consisted of 29 students. The sample comprised of boys in the age group of 13-14 years. It was found that ITM and AOM were more effective than conventional teaching in terms of improving students achievement and that pupils reacted favorably toward ITM and AOM.

Sushma(1987) investigated the effect of Concept Attainment Model(CAM) and Biological Science Inquiry Model(BSIM) for teaching biological sciences on achievement and attitude to science and also compared their effectiveness. 78 standard eighth girl students were selected using purposive sampling technique. One experimental group was taught by CAM and the other experimental group by BSIM. The control group was taught by traditional approach. Both the models were found to be effective. The CAM was found to be more effective when compared with BSIM and BSIM found to be more effective than Conventional teaching with reference to changing the attitude favorably and improving their achievement level.

Agarwal, R. and Mishra, K.S.(1988) studied the effectiveness of the reception strategy of Concept Attainment Model in enhancing the attainment of science concepts and found it to be effective.

Kaushik, N.K.(1988) has investigated the long term effect of advance organisers on achievement in Biology in relation to reading ability, intelligence and scientific attitude of the learners. It was found that the general introduction or an overview, which generally precedes learning material, is less effective when compared to advance organisers.

Sau, T.(1988) conducted a critical review of some researches on Information Processing Model of teaching. The findings of the study indicated that most of the studies were unidimensional, although the concept was multidimensional.

Baveja. B.(1989a, 1989b) conducted two comparative studies to investigate the effectiveness of Concept Attainment Model with Taba's Inductive Thinking Model in regard to concept learning in biology and also analysed the thinking strategies used by the learners. The two studies had different sample population and elaboration. The findings of both the studies support the role of inductive thinking processes in the process conceptualisation and generalisation.

Chaudhury, K.(1989) investigated and found that the

teaching skills and competence developed among student teachers through the use of Concept Attainment Model(CAM) are easily transferable in other teaching situations, besides the teaching of concepts. This study also recommended the use of CAM technique to develop the teaching skills.

Singh, D.K.((1990) investigated the effect of Inquiry Training Model and Concept Attainment Model over traditional teaching methods for teaching physical sciences. It was found that both the models were equally effective in teaching of physical science to class IX pupils.

Sood, K.(1990) conducted a comparative study on effectiveness of Advance Organizer Model (AOM) and Concept Attainment Model(CAM) for acquisition of language concepts in relation to cognitive style, intelligence and creativity. It was found that CAM was more effective than AOM in teaching of concepts in Hindi. Intelligence, creative levels and cognitive style were redundant factors so far as the learning of concepts were concerned.

Gupta, S.(1991) conducted an experimental study on the effectiveness of Ausbel's Advance Organizer Model(AOM) in developing teaching competence of student teachers and their attitude towards teaching. It was found that AOM was effective in developing teaching competence among student teachers under simulated as well as classroom conditions.

Jamini (1991) took up a study with an objective to investigate the relative effect of Advance Organiser Model (AOM) and Concept Attainment Model (CAM) on conceptual learning efficiency and retention of Chemistry concepts in relation to divergent thinking. The findings indicated that although both AOM and CAM were equally effective in fostering concept learning, the AOM was comparatively more beneficial to pupils with high divergent thinking while CAM with low divergent thinking pupils. AOM was found to be more effective than CAM in the retention of concepts irrespective of the level of divergent thinking.

Kaur.R.P.(1991) investigated the effectiveness of Bruner's Concept Attainment Model(CAM) and Ausbel's Advance Organizer Model(AOM) for teaching of economics to high and low achieving students across creativity levels. It was found that for teaching of economics both the models are effective and that AOM is more effective than CAM. The interaction between teaching strategies, intelligence and creativity were not found to be significant.

Manocha.V.(1991) studied Reception and Selection strategy in comparison to the conventional method of teaching of concepts in Biology. The findings indicated that there is no significant difference between Reception and Selection strategies with respect to achievement scores.

Pal and Misra(1991) investigated the effect of Jurisprudential strategy of teaching on development of social consciousness and ability to solve value conflicts among pupils of class IX. It was found that the individual Jurisprudential Inquiry Approach was less effective than the group approach.

Pandey SP(1991) studied the instructional and nurturant effects of Jurisprudential Inquiry Model. It was found that intelligence and the socioeconomic status of pupils interacted with the development of certain values such as equality, tolerance and justice.

Khan and Siddiqui(1992) reviewed the studies on effectiveness of Concept Attainment Strategies. It came up with the findings that concept attainment strategies were more effective over the traditional approach and attainment of disjunctive concepts is more difficult than the attainment of conjunctive concepts.

Mahajan(1992) took up a comparative study of

effectiveness of two models of teaching viz., Bruner's Concept Attainment Model (CAM) and Ausubels' Advance Organizer Model (AOM) on teaching abilities of student teachers and on achievement of students in various schools. It was found that the group taught by CAM was superior to groups taught by AOM as well as the routine method as far as the teaching ability of student teachers is concerned.

Mohanty (1992) compared Jurisprudential Inquiry Model (JIM) with Concept Attainment Model (CAM) in development of moral concepts and judgement and personal values of class VIII pupils. The findings of the study indicated JIM was more effective for developing the moral judgement and personal values of students whereas CAM was effective in developing moral concepts.

Joshi, Anuradha et al. (1993) took an experimental study to find the impact of Concept Attainment Model on general mental ability of social science students. It was found that mean general mental ability scores of students taught through Concept Attainment Model was significantly higher than those taught through traditional method.

Panda B.B.(1994) attempted to ascertain the effectiveness of Advance Organiser Model (AOM) and Set Induction(SI) in enhancing learning retention and transfer. The study intended to find the effect of AOM and Set Induction on learning of class IX, to compare the effectiveness of AOM and Traditional Method (TM) and set induction and TM, AOM and SI on achievement and to determine the influence of interaction between methods of instruction, sex and criterion test. The sample of the study comprised of 69 students of class IX of a school. The data were collected using General Mental Ability Test of Jalota and criterion test developed by the researcher and were treated with Mean, SD, three-way ANOVA and t-test . It was found that students studying through AOM and SI scored higher than traditional method. There was no interaction between methods of instruction, sex and immediate and delayed test, and there was no significant difference between achievement of boys and girls.

Singh S.N.(1994) in his study investigated the effectiveness of Inductive Thinking Model(ITM) in comparison to Traditional Method(TM) of teaching economics to class XI. The study intended to study the effectiveness of ITM in terms of achievement in economics as well as reaction of students towards ITM, to compare ITM with TM in terms of achievement, inductive reasoning, concept formation, higher mental ability in economics, scientific attitude and creativity separately by considering intelligence, achievement motivation as co-variates, to study the effect of treatment, sex and their interaction on the dependent variables separately. The sample comprised of 350 class XI students. It was found that ITM was more effective compared to TM in terms of achievement in economics and reaction towards ITM. Intelligence significantly influenced the dependent variables. Interaction between treatment and sex influenced the achievement. ITM was suitable for both male and female students in teaching economics in comparison to traditional method.

Ajatha Swamy(1995) compared the effectiveness of Inquiry Training Model (ITM) and Conventional Method(CM) of teaching science in terms of (i) developing science process skills (ii) fostering fluency, flexibility and orginality components of creativity (iii) boosting curiosity and to investigate the interaction between treatments and levels with reference to the dependent variables.. The sample consisted of 36 matched pairs of students with one as the control group and the other the experimental group. The tool used for collecting data were Verbal Test of Creative Thinking of Baqer Mehdi, Science Process Skills Test and Curiosity Test by the investigator. The data collected were analysed by two-way ANOVA, Scheffe's test and t-test. It was found that ITM was more effective than CM in developing science process skills for above average and below average groups. ITM was more effective than CM in fostering fluency and originality components of creativity. ITM was more effective than CM in boosting curiosity. It was also found that the students sustained the skills developed, curiosity boosted and creativity fostered through ITM of teaching science.

Naresh Kumar Gupta(1995) studied the relative effectiveness of Some Information Processing Models of teaching (i.e. Concept Attainment Model(CAM), Inductive Thinking model(IThM) and Inquiry Training Model(ITM) on mental processes and attitudes towards science. A purposive sample of 140 students in the form of three non equivalent intact sections of class IX in same school were drawn by incidental sampling technique. The tools used were Group General Mental Ability Test by S.Jalota, Reasoning Ability Test (RAT) by K. Bayati, Passi's tests of creativity, science attitude scale by Avinash Grewal and Verbal test of scientific creativity by V.P. Sharma and J.P. Shukla. Quasi-experimental method was employed in a natural setting with pre-test and post-test parallel group design. It was found that CAM was effective in developing reasoning ability, scientific creativity whereas it could not foster inquisitiveness, persistency of problem awareness among the students. Inductive Thinking Model promoted reasoning ability, scientific creativity, problem awareness ability but could not bring significant enhancement in inquisitiveness. ITM was effective in developing reasoning ability, scientific creativity, problem awareness ability, however it could not bring significant gain in inquisitiveness and persistency. CAM , ITM and Inductive Thinking Model did not differ in effectiveness in terms of enhancing reasoning ability or scientific creativity. ITM and Inductive Thinking Model rated better than CAM in fostering problem awareness ability. However Inductive Thinking Model and ITM did not differ in fostering seeing the problem ability.

Anandi Martis(1999) took up an action research study

to find the effect of Desensitization Model of teaching on fears of adolescent boys of a local school. It aimed at preparing lessons for sessions on Desensitization model of teaching and to find the effect of it on the scores of fears measured by the Fear Survey Scale. Action research methodology with a single group pretest-posttest research design was used. 300 adolescent boys of standard IX were surveyed on a Fear survey scale. Sixty adolescent boys were selected as the sample for the experiment. It was found that the model of teaching helped in reducing fear.

2.2 Training for use of Models of Teaching

Passi Singh and Sansanwal(1985) developed a training strategy for models of teaching. The objectives of the study were to study the effectiveness of Concept Attainment Model(CAM) and Inquiry Training Model(ITM) in terms of (a) understanding of the model (b) reaction towards the model (c) to study the resultant willingness of teacher educators to implement the models in teacher education programmes (d) to develop a strategy of training in models of teaching. 45 teacher educators representing 25 institutions from nine states and five union territories were selected by purposive sampling. The teacher educators were invited to attend an 8-day workshop on Models of teaching held at Devi Ahilya Vishwavidyalay, Indore in April 1985. Single group pretest post-test design was employed. The treatment comprised of orientation in the theory of model, a lesson plan guide and a teacher analysis guide, through lectures and discussion. This was followed by demonstration lessons and practice. The tools used were, theory check-up for CAM and ITM by Joyce and Weil at Indore and reaction scale for CAM and ITM and willingness scale for implementation of models developed for the study. It was found that training in CAM and ITM comprising lecture demonstration, discussion and peer practice plus feed back enhanced the understanding, of teacher educator's theoretical aspects of CAM and ITM. The training strategy was found effective in terms of developing understanding, favorable reaction and willingness to implement models of teaching in a teacher training programme.

Das,B.C(1993) studied the effectiveness of CAM in terms of (i) teaching competencies of pre-service student-teachers (ii) understanding the model (iii) training the model (iv) coaching the model & (v)reaction towards the model at various stages of training. The sample of the study comprised of sixteen students-teachers studying in B.Ed. of the department of education(belonging to Devi Ahilya Vishwavidyalay). Tools used were theory check-up test by Bruce Joyce, Modified theory check-up by Sansanwal ,Reaction scale by B.K. Passi and Sansanwal, teaching analysis guide by Bruce Joyce. It was found that CAM was effective in developing teaching competencies of pre-service student-teachers. The training given to student-teachers increased understanding about theoretical aspects of CAM. The training affected the teaching behaviors of student-teachers at coaching stage. CAM was effective in terms of training. The training process from theory to practice had brought significant changes in student-teachers reaction towards CAM.

2.3 Developing Models for Teaching

Exemmal.J(1980) constructed certain models for teaching school botany using environmental and ethnic resources. The efficacy of such models was tested by comparing the achievement in botany. He compared the effectiveness of environmental approach and the formal approach in realizing certain educational outcomes. The effect of environmental approach on the attitude of pupil towards teaching and learning was also examined. The tools employed were teaching models in botany, a rating scale on teaching models, achievement test in botany, attitude towards science teaching and learning, judgement schedule for teachers and students, verbal intelligence test and a science interest inventory. This was an experimental study limited to eight schools. Six topics of botany of standard IX were selected for construction of teaching models. The findings indicated that the environmental approach was superior to formal approach in stimulating cognitive growth in pupils, in developing interests in scientific activities and in scoring high marks. Environmental approach was significantly superior to formal approach in terms of immediate post-teaching and delayed memory scores.

Hymavathi.K.(1993) evolved a new teaching model for developing the effective aspects of children of 5 to 8 years. The objectives were to define affective domain in terms of functional behavior, to develop and consolidate approaches for developing affective functional behavior into a model form, to implement, verify its validity and to improve the model for implementation at the National level. The sample comprised of five experimental schools with 100 students and five control schools with 100 students from class 1 to III. Rating scale and interview schedule were used as tools. It was found that the affective functional behavior could be developed through various activities and methods that are practicable in schools.

2.4 Fostering Creativity

Some of the important milestones in creativity research are programmes for stimulating creativity like Synectics(Gordon 1971), Brainstorming(Osborn 1971), Attribute listing(Crawford 1954), Morphological analysis(Zwicky 1969) and many others. In the present review, studies related to techniques for stimulating creativity have been emphasized owing to the nature of investigation.

Torrance(1964) cites the study of Anderson(1963) in which the investigator employed three conditions, sample being a class of general education course in industrial arts. In addition to usual control condition and in the other he merely handed out from time to time sheets giving information about the creative process, becoming more creative and the like. No classroom time was devoted to the discussion of these sheets. Any discussion that was held was among the students and on their own time outside class. Students in this later condition showed significantly greater growth in measured creative thinking abilities than their peers who had not been given these handouts.

Covington and Crutch field(1965) have devised auto-instructional programmes composed of detective and mystery story materials for fifth and sixth grade children. The results revealed that the subjects who used the programmes markedly performed better than the control subjects on certain problem-solving, creativity and relevant attitude measures.

Oltan(1967) investigated mainly the extent to which thinking and problem-solving of fifth grade students could be improved by the use of self-instructional programmed lessons (The productive thinking programme). The sample included 704 students. The results showed statistically significant increments in thinking and problem solving performance on a wide variety of productivity thinking measures. These instructional benefits occurred for virtually all types of students regardless of sex or general IQ level, and were especially marked for students in classrooms having environments which were providing little support and encouragement for the development of productivity thinking.

Shackel and Lawrence(1969) developed an auto-instructional programme that attempted to increase the factors of creativity, viz. fluency, flexibility, originality and elaboration. They found that the six programmed text books, they devised were effective.

Wardrop and others (1969) developed self-instructional programmed lessons and conducted a controlled experiment in 44 fifth grade classrooms to investigate the extent to which creativity and problem solving skills of children could be nurtured through these self instructional programmed lessons. Experimental group which received the programmed lessons scored significantly high in creativity and problem solving skills. Improvements in productive thinking skills were found for both boys and girls of both higher and lower IQ.

Davis(1971) developed a programme in the form of dialogues among four characters, a scientist-inventor, a relative of a famous secret spy and others, with the humor as an ingredient. The characters try to become idea-finders and use 'attribute listing', 'morphological synthesis', 'checklist procedure' and 'Synectics'. The report of the investigation indicated that 23 students who used the programme produced 65 percent more ideas on three divergent thinking tasks than 32 control students.

John.E.Penic(1973) studied the effect of two patterns of training on aspects of verbal and figural creativity in fifth grade science students. This was a single group study. The training patterns are Student-Structured Learning in Science(SSLS) and Teacher Structured Learning in Science(TSLS). It was found that there was no significant difference in verbal creativity between the two groups.

Torrance and Torrance(1973) in their review of 142 studies have considered twenty-five experimental studies involving complex programmes with packaged instructional materials. The three main programmes have been (i) the Covington, Crutch field and Davies Productive thinking programme, (ii) the purdue creative thinking programme, and (iii) the Myers and Torrance idea books. In the evaluations, each of these sets of materials scores fairly well, especially when there is class and teacher involvement in their use. The 'percentage success' for these and other programmes together has been 72 percent.

Allencar(1974) studied the effects of the purdue creative thinking programme on pupils creative thinking abilities of fourth and fifth grades of public and private schools of Brazil. The children in the experimental groups heard story of a famous American pioneer from the teacher and worked on some creativity exercises. It was found that the programme had a positive effect on the development of pupil's creative thinking abilities. The experimental group outscored the control group on the Torrance tests of creative thinking.

Johnson(1975) studied the effects of special guided lessons in creative thinking prepared with the help of classroom ideas for encouraging thinking and feeling by Williams(1970), upon the creative thinking ability of randomly selected 353 fourth grade students in twenty classrooms. He also investigated differences in creative thinking abilities between male and female experimental subjects. Significant F-ratio was got in favor of experimental group on total creative thinking, as well as on the tests of flexible thinking and elaborate thinking. An analysis of variance between experimental boys and girls revealed a significantly high F-ratio for girls on total creative thinking and on the test of flexible thinking.

Sharpe(1975) tried to enhance the verbal and figural creative abilities of Educationally Handicapped(EH) children, using brainstorming and programmed instruction techniques, Nine intermediate EH classes were randomly assigned to four experimental treatments viz., i) brainstorming ii) programmed instruction iii) combination of brainstorming and programmed instruction and iv) control. The programme lasted for eight weeks. Alternative forms of Torrance tests of creative thinking (TTCT) were administered as pre and post tests. Post hoc tests of significance showed that the brainstorming group scored significantly higher than the programmed instruction and control groups on verbal fluency and verbal flexibility. The same group scored significantly higher than the programmed instructional group on verbal originality. The three experimental groups scored significantly higher than the control group on figural fluency. Only brainstorming group scored significantly higher than the control group on figural flexibility. There were no significant differences between the treatment groups on figural originality or figural elaboration.

Blankenship(1976) investigated the effects of ten hours of creativity training comprising fifteen activities, upon the creativity performance, achievement and self-concept of first graders. Four classes, each of twenty four students were randomly assigned to an experimental and a control group, with two in each school. The pre-test and post-test parallel group design was used. The analysis of variance indicated that the experimental subjects made significant improvements on fluency, flexibility, originality and elaboration. The control group did not improve significantly on any of the variables.

Nirpharake(1977) took up training of VII standard students in a study. This was pretest, post-test matched group study of six groups consisting of six boys each. One was control group, whereas the remaining four took one programme each viz., training in creative perception, training in divergent production, training in creative appreciation and training in creative problem solving, the sixth group were trained in all the four areas. The training programmes appreciably improved the creative thinking of the subjects on Torrance Tests of Creative Thinking(TTCT). Training in the areas other than divergent production contributed significantly in the improvement. The group which had training in all the four areas scored higher than the remaining groups.

Organ(1977) in her study had eighty second and third grade children ranging in age from 7.6 to 9.6 years, who were randomly placed in two groups, experimental (twenty girls and twenty boys), control group(twenty girls and twenty boys).The experimental subjects were introduced to a creative thought production instructional programme, which composed of (i) a time period for discussion and (ii) a presentation of motivational model charts developed by the investigator and administered by four trained research assistants. The control group received a comparable period of group discussion and visual situation, without systematized instruction by the class teacher. The programme lasted for five weeks of forty minutes per day. The children were pre-tested and post-tested on figural forms, A and B of Torrance test of Creative thinking(TTCT). By analysis of variance it was found that there was significant difference on fluency, flexibility, originality and elaboration scores between the experimental and control groups with different programmes. There was no significant sex difference and there was no significant interaction between the sex and treatment on each of the four measures of creative thinking.

Sunaree(1977) prepared lesson plans, based on William's Cognitive Affective Teaching Model to foster creative abilities of children. Eighteen plans were developed, each one on paradoxes, attributes, analogies etc. for VII standard children of Thailand. All of them are culture-free and could be used in Indian Classrooms also.

Williams(1977) while reviewing the studies, reports that purdue creative thinking programme developed by Feldhusen, et. al. (1970) has been found effective in studies by Bahlke(1967) and Feldhusen, Bahlke and Treffinger(1969).

Davis and Bull(1978) in their study on two groups of eighty seven and sixty undergraduate students provided a five week course which was a mixture of academic material and hands-on involvement activities. The course included topics such as creative and problem solving process, the creative personality, creative dramatics, creative thinking techniques, brainstorming etc. Class A took 'How do you think' (HDYT) on the first day and 'Adjective Checklist' (ACL) on the last day. Conversely class B took ACL on first day and HDYT on the last day. For both groups the trained subjects scored significantly higher than their respective before training controls. In both the groups the training effects was stronger for females than males. The ACL-creativity appeared to be more sensitive to creativity training which may be due to the large number of biographical items in HDYT.

Pillay.G.S.(1978) studied the effects of patterns of teaching upon creative thinking among adolescents. The objectives of the study were to find out the effect of Creative Teaching Method(CTM) (combination of morphological analysis, brainstorming and traditional method) on general creative ability, on creativity in geography and achievement in geography. The study employed multifactor co-variance design having experimental and control groups. The sample consisted of seventy one eighth grade students(36 control and 35 experimental group). Madhookar Intelligence test, and Passi's test of creativity were used as tools. Creative thinking in geography and achievement were tested by tools developed by the investigator. The findings indicated that the CTM when compared to traditional method did not produce differential effect upon general creative thinking and on creative thinking in geography too. Out of thirty mental abilities, seven were developed significantly by CTM whereas memory for word meanings was improved by traditional method.

Schneider(1978) took eighteen activities from the talent areas of productive thinking for treatment and forecasting for a nine week period. 191 fifth and sixth grade pupils from six rural elementary schools formed the sample. The experimental group consisted of forty males and fifty eight females and control group fifty one males and forty two females. Torrance test of Creative Thinking (TTCT) and Coppersmith self-esteem inventory was used for pre-test and post-test. The major conclusions were (i) the activities employed in this study can effect significant gains in flexibility and total creativity scores, but not on fluency and originality , (ii) the activities had no effect on self-esteem scores and (iii) girls at the fifth and sixth grade levels scored higher on verbal creativity measures than boys.

Deshmukh(1979) studied the relative effectiveness of brainstorming and role playing techniques in the secondary school children of Nagpur. It was found that brainstorming was relatively superior to role playing in terms of significant differences on the creativity tests. The investigator also surveyed the instruction in schools, to find out the plug points, where creativity fostering could be put.

Jaben(1980) stimulated the creative thinking of learning disabled experimental children, using the Purdue Creative Thinking Programme, comprising twenty eight audiotapes and exercises aimed to develop divergent thinking. A group of learning disabled control children and another group of normal children acted as the control group. A clinical problem-solving task was administered as a post test to ascertain the effectiveness of the creativity training to extend the problem solving skills along with a different form of Torrance tests of creative thinking(TTCT). Analysis of the data revealed that learning disabled children can be taught creative verbal behaviors as measured by TTCT, and that creativity training effectively extended to problem solving skills as measured by problem-solving task.

Teeling(1980) studied the effect of a process approach to teaching creativity on the creative thinking performance of third and fifth grade students. Multiple talent approach was employed for teaching. The sample consisted of 226 third and fifth graders. Pre-test, Post-test control group design was used. The major conclusions were: (i) the girls appear to benefit more than boys from the multiple talent approach to teaching; (ii) fifth grade students appear to benefit more than the third grade students; and (iii) the creativity test score gains favoring the experimental students seem to justify the conclusions that it is potentially possible to enhance creative thinking through a teaching process.

Jerial(1981) took immediate problems(verbal and non verbal) of the environment, some divergent and some convergent and developed twenty five lesson plans. Each lesson had four steps viz., preliminary work, introduction, statement of the problem and exercises. The item was presented on the first day and the discussion was held on the second day. Gains on Torrance Test of Creativity thinking (TTCT) form B, were highly significant compared to form A.

Shah(1981) conducted an experimental investigation of the effects of four selected teaching strategies on development of creative thinking and achievement in science. Four groups of students of seventh grade and four student-teachers were selected for the experiment. A 4 X 4 latin square design was used for the study. These groups were taught by selected teachers for fourteen weeks. It was found that the four strategies of teaching had significantly differential effects on the development of originality and flexibility but not in the case of fluency. The effects of strategies were dependent upon the level of intelligence, sex and creativeness of pupils. The results also highlighted the importance of maximum use of audio-visual aids in classroom teaching for enhancement of creative thinking.

Upadhya.R.(1981) undertook a study to find the effect of stimulating environment on change in creativity ability of young children. This was an experimental study with twin group pretest-post test design. 400 students of three to six years of age were selected using random sampling techniques. Creativity test for pre-schools was developed by the researcher. It was found that stimulating environment significantly increased the creativity scores of the experimental group in all three dimensions of creativity viz., fluency, flexibility and originality.

Bhaskara.S.(1982) studied the effectiveness of self developed verbal creativity instructional materials at school stage. 570 students of sixth grade from two urban and two rural schools formed the sample. Passi's test of verbal creativity translated to kannada was used. It was found that the creativity instructional materials were able to increase the creative thinking abilities. Urban students were better than rural and boys were better than girls in terms of gain scores of creativity tests.

Mohmed Miyan(1982) undertook a study to examine the effectiveness of methods of teaching mathematics in developing mathematical creativity. The sample comprised of students of three sections of class ninth of a school. Test of mathematical creativity developed by the investigator was used for both pre-test and post-test. It was found that none of the three methods was significantly different in developing mathematical creativity. The guided discovery method was most effective in enhancing originality compared with tell and do and pure discovery methods.

Carter Lindakay(1983) studied the effect of multimodel creativity training on creativity of twelfth graders. The sample comprised of forty eight students of a school. Torrance test of creative thinking and interviews were used for final assessment. This experimental study followed the twin group-control experimental, pre-test post-test design. It was concluded that the treatment did not significantly improve the creativity of the students.

Vora, Gira C.(1984) investigated the impact of Divergent Thinking Programme in Mathematics (DTPM) on creative levels of the children of seventh and eighth classes. The investigator constructed the divergent thinking programme consisting of three types of problems i) multi response type ii) hidden shape type iii) make-up problem type. The sample comprised of 271 students - 130 students of seventh and 141 students of eighth grade. The findings indicated that the experimental group was superior in fluency and originality-components of creativity for both the grades. The programme worked well for both high and low creative students.

Gupta. P.K.(1985) developed and evaluated a creative training programme(CTP) for sixth grade children and studied the interaction effect of intelligence and sex with CTP on fluency, flexibility, originality and composite creativity. The sample comprised of 357 students (188 girls and 169 boys). The tools used were Jalota's Group test of general intelligence and Baqer Mehdi's tests of creative thinking. It was found that CTP was successful in developing creative thinking abilities. CTP was equally effective for both boys and girls. There was no significant interaction between intelligence, sex and CTP for any of the components of creativity.

Singh. B.D.(1985) took up a study to find the effect of a specially designed teaching strategy and some socio physiological factors on creativity among middle school children. The sample consisted of 277 male students of class seventh and eight grades. Mathematical creativity test and General creativity test by Baqer Mehdi and Thorondike's dimensions of temperament test was used before and after treatment. The main findings of the study indicated that the specially designed teaching strategy had a significant effect of different dimensions of creativity. The high and low general creative did not significantly differ with reference to ten personality factors measured by Thorondike's dimensions of temperament.

Below Mary Eleanor(1986) examined the effects of creative reading materials when used by teachers with varying degree of creative attitude on creative thinking skills of the student. The materials were designed by the researcher. The sample consisted of 267 fourth grade students divided into experimental and control group. Pre-test post-test design was used. Torrance tests of creative thinking was used. It was found that post test mean scores were significantly high in the experimental group. It indicated that a teacher with a high creative attitude trained in creativity and who used creativity training materials of her own design can be influential in affecting child's creative thinking skills.

Patel. J.Z.(1987) investigated the effectiveness of the purdue creative thinking programme on creative abilities of elementary school children. Eight classes of different schools selected were equated on basis of scores on creative ability tests by J.Z. Patel. Four classes formed experimental classes where programmes were implemented and remaining four classes formed the control classes. The programme was translated into Gujrati. The effect of training on experimental group was found to be significant for creativity and its two components viz. fluency and originality. The main effect of IQ was significant but sex was not significant.

Ryar Micheal.V.(1988) prepared and tried out a non-verbal and verbal programme for developing creative thinking ability (CTA) in the students of the age group 10+ and 12+ controlling some psycho-socio factors. The sample comprised of 330 fifth, sixth and seventh grade students selected from three schools. Two experimental groups and one control group was formed. Intervening variables were controlled using ANCOVA. Verbal and non-verbal creative thinking ability criterion tests developed by the investigator was used. It was found that experimental groups gained by CTA. The CTA treatment was more effective when different variables like anxiety, parental behavior, self-done activities, school achievement, self-sufficiency, neuroticism, emotional stability and IQ were controlled.

Gulati, Sushma(1995) conducted a study to analyse how instructional materials helped children's creativity in class room and its effectiveness in fostering creativity. The sample comprised of students of class fifth. Alternate uses test of Guilford, Parallel lines of Torrance and Unusual uses and circle of Torrance and a questionnaire were used to collect data. It was found that the difference between mean scores of pre-test and post-test were consistently significant both in case of flexibility and orginality.

Some studies aimed at finding out whether or not the students from academic streams, namely, science, arts, home science and commerce differ among themselves with reference to creativity. Srivastava and Jha(1977) and Srivastava(1978) reported that the science students were superior, to arts and commerce students as far as their achievement in creativity is concerned. Science students were found to be significantly higher than arts students in fluency, flexibility components of creativity(Awasty 1979). In non-verbal creativity too, science students were found to be superior to arts students, but in verbal creativity arts students were significantly superior to science students (Jarial 1981). Kaur(1980) observed that commerce students were significantly superior to science and home-science students in verbal creativity, while science students scored significantly higher than the home science students in verbal creativity. No significant difference in verbal creativity was found between the group of arts and science students (Rawat and Garg, 1977), between arts and commerce students(Srivastava and Jha, 1977) and between science and commerce students (Sansanwal and Jarial, 1979). From the available evidences, it may be concluded that students from arts, science, home-science and commerce streams differ among themselves in creativity.

2.5 Inducing Problem Solving Ability

Parnes(1971) discusses in detail, the procedure of creative problem solving course at the University of Buffalo. The pupils were taught the technique of brainstorming in detail, with the use of check list procedures and forced fit techniques. Importance of record keeping, deferred judgement, free wheeling etc. are stressed and informal procedures are used in the training. Analysis of the results indicate that i) the creative problem solving students show substantial gain in quantity of ideas on two tests, than the control group ii) on three tests of idea quality, the creative problem solving students showed clear superiority but on a fourth test the difference was not significant iii) on three tests of personality to measure 'self-control' and 'need to achieve' the creative problem solving students gained substantial dominance, but showed no significant changes in 'self-control' or 'need to achieve'.

Torrance and Torrance(1973) in their review of 142 studies provide 91 percent success for Osborn-Parnes Creative Problem-solving course and/or modifications. The reasons for the success of creative problem solving courses are: i) the problem solving is very much similar to the creative thought process itself; ii) the solving of creative problems are enjoyed by the children because of the novelty of the problems.

Biles (1977) took forty graduate and professional students and randomly assigned them to two groups. Twenty three subjects took the creative problem-solving course based on the text book by Osborn (1971) and the work book by Parnes (1967) for ten hours. The Torrance Tests of Creative Thinking (TTCT) were selected as the criterion for evaluating the outcomes of the course and the two forms were used. The experimental subjects benefited from the experience in terms of significant improvement on scores for two of the three verbal factors and one of the four figural factors.

Kealey(1977) used a pre-test, post-test control group design with eighteen foreign language student teachers at Ohio University. The experimental treatment received by the group A, consisted of a six week abbreviated version of Parnes(1967) creative problem solving course. The control condition A2, consisted of seminar sessions in which specific student teaching problems were discussed. Verbal creativity was measured by Torrance Tests of Creative Thinking (TTCT) and operation creativity, by student ratings on a tool developed by the investigators. Results indicated no significant differences between groups on either TTCT or on student ratings, but significant correlation existed between the two, Torrance tests and student ratings.

Jain S.C.(1982) studied the problem solving behavior in Physics among certain groups of adolescent pupils. He studied the need for selected hints, at various stages of problem solving and the problem solving ability of adolescent pupils, boys and girls at high, average and low creativity levels. A sample of 180 pupils (90 boys and 90 girls) of class XI(Science) was selected randomly. Creativity was measured by Baqer Medhi Verbal test of creativity. Ten problems in Physics based on different reasoning patterns were arbitrarily framed to measure problem solving ability. The findings indicated that the hints when presented systematically and logically were helpful in making the students conscious about the analysis of the problem and recalling of the relevant knowledge, and to some extent for the correct use of reasoning patterns. No significant differences for problem solving ability scores were observed among the three groups differing in creativity.

Rai(1982) has studied the process of problem solving in creative science and non-creative science students. Two groups of creative and non-creative students identified by creativity Test of Mehdi, totaling 200 of Patna were tested on problem solving in the same conditions. It was found that creative children need more tasks as assignments in their curriculum.

Talegaonkar(1984) developed teaching strategies with the purpose of encouraging students for problems solving in science creativity. The sample included 34 students of IX class of Pune. Pre-test post-test matched group design was adopted. Different strategies employed for improvement of creativity were creative problem solving, games observation, question storming, group discussions, laboratory work and supply of instructional materials to students. Two self made verbal tests highlighting fluency, flexibility and originality was used to find difference shown in abilities to solve problem creatively. One was used as pretest and the other as post test. These tests were not standardized. Training was given for 18 hours and extended over a period of six months. Data was analysed qualitatively through graphic representations and through median test. The findings indicated that there was no significant increase in their ability of lateral thinking of the students, but they responded well during the conduct of the experiment. The students could not reach the final solution due to lack of time and equipment for experimentation.

Kumari.U.M.C.(1993) tested various methods of problem solving with guided-discovery. The students were exposed to tasks and problems and were encouraged to produce a large number of creative solutions. Creative problem solving ability was measured with the help of a realistic and interesting test. The results of the study supported the hypotheses regarding the usefulness of guided discovery methods and educational materials across different types of assessment tools and samples.

2.6 Role of Analogies in Learning

Royer and Cable (1976) found that analogies were only employed when the target was difficult to understand, i.e., when students felt that it was necessary to look for analogies as an aid to understanding.

Khatena Joe(1977) reports that through a special training programme, the experimental group was taught to use simile, metaphor, personification and allusion as comparison forms within the four analogy classifications, viz. , Direct Personal, Symbolic and Fantasy analogy to differentiate between simple and complex images in the production of analogies. Generally high and low creative experimentals obtained significant originality scores than high and low creative controls; experimental and controls preferred to use direct analogy, simple image patterns to other analogy -image forms; and high creatives of both groups produced more complex images than the low creatives of both the groups; and only one symbolic analogy and a few fantasy analogies were produced by both the groups, with experimentals producing more fantasy analogies than the controls. Although the training programme significantly increased mean originality scores, it did not serve the function of significantly increasing the use of personal, fantasy and symbolic analogies.

Enyeart (1979) for instance, found no general correlation between analogy use and Paigetian levels. There was only a significant correlation between the use of formal analogies (i.e., analogies representing proportions) and formal operation thought. Gabel and Sherwood (1980) reported a tendency for their analogies to be more effective for students of lower formal reasoning ability and not especially useful for more capable students.

Gentner and Gentner (1983) reported that analogies aided problem solving in the area of the electric circuit. They further showed that the analogy employed considerably influenced the problem-solving process. They found that problem solving in the area of the electrical circuit among college and high school students was considerably different from when a "flowing fluid" or a "moving crowd" analogy was used. These findings point to the fact that the general framework that the analogy provides has a significant influence on the learning process.

Curtis and Reigeluth (1984) analysed analogy use in 26 science text books. The use of analogies according to several categories (such as type of analogy or placement) was investigated. In total, 216 analogies were found i.e. 8.3

analogies per book (ranging from zero to 18). Two main types of analogy were distinguished, namely, simpler ones based mainly on surface similarities and more elaborate ones based on what Curtis and Reigeluth called "functional relationships". In total, most analogies were of the latter kind (70%). Whereas this number was less than 50% in elementary books, it was substantially higher in chemistry and physics books (about 90%). This result points in a similar direction to that of Glynn et al.(1989) who found that elaborate analogies were most often used in physics textbooks. It is interesting that in about 50% of the 216 analogies, the authors made no attempt to describe the analogy or how to strategically use the analogies provided. There are similar findings in the study of Glynn et al. (1989); guidance toward effective use of analogies was not explicitly given in the introduction of the text books. Curtis and Reigeluth (1984) drew several conclusions from their study that may help to produce powerful analogies. They point out that analogies appear to be most useful for complex and difficult content. They view simpler analogies that are mainly based on surface similarities as only suitable for easier, more concrete topics, whereas more difficult and abstract topics require functional analogies, i.e., analogies based on deep structure similarities.

Gentner and Landers (1985) investigated access to analogies. These findings reconfirm on the one hand the results by Tenney and Gentner (1985) that the inferential power of analogies is governed by similarities of higher-order structure. On the other hand, they found that accessibility is governed by literal or surface similarities but not by similarities from higher-order structures.

Tenny and Gentner (1985) summarised findings of studies for water analogies of the electric circuit. Increased familiarity with the base domain was not sufficient to ensure the discovery of a potentially useful analogy. However, increased, familiarity did improve the usefulness of the analogy if detected. The results suggest that familiarity with the base domain affects the power rather than the accessibility of an analogy.

Holyoak and Koh(1987) also investigated the influence of structural and surface similarities on access to analogies . They found that both similarities are influential but they did not conclude that surface ones govern access. However, they agree with Gentner and Landers (1985) in that only structural similarities affected student's ability to make use of an analog domain once its relevance was pointed out.

Clement (1987) has studied the spontaneous use of analogies in a systematic manner. He investigated, for instance, how novices and experts employ analogies when solving physics problems. The main findings are that both novices and experts frequently make spontaneous use of analogies or at least of comparisons. The studies, therefore, reconfirm that analogies are common tools for explaining and trying to make sense of the unknown.

Black and Solomon(1987) for instance, investigated student's use of analogies for electrical current. They found that the analogies presented helped students to learn. They interpreted this finding from a constructive view ; analogies were helpful because they allowed the students to construct their own knowledge by forcing them to view the new knowledge within the frame work of the analogy.

Segre and Giani(1987) summarized their findings on analogical reasoning about transport processes in the following way: "Our students are almost unable to employ analogical reasoning to solve similar problems regarding different phenomenologies in the field of transport processes". They thought a lack of their student's ability to "formalize" was responsible for their negative results. Clement stated that attempts to use analogies in learning situations did not work because the learners were not able to "see" the analogy.

Research on student's conceptions supports these findings in so far as areas that are seen as obviously similar by the teacher(or scientist) are viewed as being fundamentally different by many students.

Sutala and Krajcik's (1988) study points in a similar direction . They found that students with high cognitive abilities benefited more from creating their own analogical connections, whereas students with low abiltiies benefited more from having the teacher help them make the analogical connection.

Tierney(1988) observed four social studies teachers for 20 lessons. He focused on "small scale" comparisons (use of metaphors, analogies, and similes as example, or reinforcement of verbal or written explanation of content used in history lessons. Such comparisons were often employed but mostly in a limited manner : "Like comedians, these teachers went with what worked. It was clear that simply telling the story of history was insufficient. Seldom did the teachers stop to check specifically that students understood the metaphors used". Very much like analogies used by authors in text books, the teachers observed by Tierney (1988) appeared to presuppose that students were familiar with the analog domain and would use the metaphors, analogies, or similes without any guidance.

Glynn et al.(1989) examined use in an analysis of 43 elementary, high school, and college science textbooks. The analysis was of an interpretive nature, i.e., it was not based on formally developed categories. Glynn et al. found many examples of simple analogies such as "mitochondria are the powerhouse of the cell" in textbooks. Elaborate analogies, which were a paragraph or even a page long,.were relatively rare. High school physics and physical science books appeared to contain the largest number of such elaborate analogies. The frequency of analogies in the 19 physics and physical science books varied between relatively extensive and little use. There is another interesting observation. Although it was common in the introduction to provide the reader with hints as to how to use the textbooks effectively (e.g., hints about advance organisers) no mention of analogies was found there - not even in the textbooks in which excellent use of analogies was made.

In a study by Treagust et al.(1990) limited analogy use is also reported. Forty lessons by eight science teachers were observed. The study was carried out within an interpretive research framework (Erickson, 1986). Field notes of lessons and an interview with every teacher at the end of the observation period formed the basis of interpretation. Use of analogies based on structural relationships (rather than surface similarities) was the focus of the study. The teachers in this study seldom used such analogies in their teaching (in the 40 lessons observed, only eight of them were detected) and tended not to use them in an elaborated manner even when such analogies were present in the textbooks used by the class. This finding seemingly contradicts the results of the interview, which revealed that most teachers were very aware of both the benefits and limitations of analogies. But the teachers in the study seemed not to have a repertoire of good analogies and were not confident concerning the effective use of analogy. Where the broader context of analogy use within a constructivistic learning perspective is concerned, the study points out that the teachers mainly held traditional views of the learning process. Accordingly analogy use - if it occurred- was not based on a constructivistic approach to learning.

2.7 Synectics Model of Teaching

Before directly presenting the studies related to Synectics model of teaching, views of researchers about Synectics procedure of nurturing creativity has been presented. Hofland(1985) presented a paper at annual meeting of American Theater Association described that three techniques that encourage right brain dominance in the generative step of the design process were random stimulation, lateral thinking and Synectics . Passi(1985) tried Synectics at a three day workshop on college students and reported it effective. Springfield(1986) and Hartic(1986) used Synectics on upper elementary gifted students and found it effective in problem solving activity. Warute(1990) studied the effect of Synectics method and found it effective for development of scientific creativity in high school students. Kawenski-Mary(1991) in "Encouraging Creativity in Design" describes a six week course for design students called "Needs Awareness and Design" which stresses development of creative thinking skills. Here he stresses Synectics for actual problem solving and creativity. Soriano-de-Alencar, Eunece.M.L.(1993) in "Thinking in the future: The need to promote creativity in educational context", suggests the use of Synectics . Lone-Cathben and others(1994) in "Teaching strategies to facilitate learning" discusses Synectics as one of the teaching strategies.

Martis.A. , D'himaC.G.(1987) conducted an experimental study to find the effect of Synectics model on pupil's creative thinking and academic achievement in science. The sample consisted of class IX students selected randomly from two sections of an English medium school. Twin group pre-test post-test design was adopted for the experiment. Torrance tests of creative thinking and achievement test developed by the investigator were the tools used. It was found that verbal and figural creativity and academic achievement of experimental group had been significantly increased after the treatment. The difference between pre-test and post-test mean scores were significant at 0.01 level for the experimental group. The difference between pre-test and post-test mean scores of control group was also found to be significant.

Krishna Murthy.B.(1989) took up a study to find out the effectiveness of the first strategy ('making familiar strange') of Synectics model through teaching of physics in developing creative thinking ability. 40 students of a section of VIII grade of a school formed the sample. Pre-test, post-test experimental design was followed. It was found that there was a significant increase in fluency, flexibility and originality components of creativity. It was equally effective for both boys and girls.

Malhotra.S.P.(1990) has investigated the effect of Synectics model of teaching on development of language creativity in Hindi. The students after being taught through this model showed more improvement on the factors of fluency, flexibility, originality and elaboration in the various areas of language skills. The improvement had a high positive correlation with the intelligence level of the students.

Martis.A.(1990) attempted to find out the effectiveness of the Synectics model in developing 'Making Strange Familiar"(MSF) competencies and also its effectiveness in developing scientific and general creativity of graduate student teachers. It was found that the training in MSF comprising theory, discussion, demonstration and practice, developed the desired competencies and generated favorable reactions in pupil teachers as well as the high school students towards the model. The training in MSF significantly improved verbal, non-verbal and scientific flexibility and originality of trainees. These achievements of the training in MSF in turn led to the development of general and scientific creativity of school students. The findings of the study also suggested that MSF needed to be slightly modified in the light of class room situations.

Anandi and Irene(1996) undertook a study to prepare instructional materials based on Synectics model of teaching for developing creativity. The instructional materials developed were found to be effective in increasing fluency and flexibility scores of verbal creative thinking but was not effective in increasing originality scores. The worksheet of pupils were very useful for systematic presentation of matter. Besides they could be evaluated. It was found that stretching exercises are a must for Synectics approach.

Sucheta.K.(1996) studied instructional and nurturant effects of Synectics model of teaching on creative ability in Hindi and English languages. The sample comprised of 250 students in VII, VIII and IX grades. It was found that Synectics model of teaching had its effect on improvement in all four factors of language creativity i.e. fluency, flexibility, originality and elaboration. The model of teaching was effective in improving general creative capacity of the students. There was significant increase in group cohesiveness. The results were similar in all three grades.

Chandra, Vaidya, Nalakar, Mahapatra(1998) took up an experimental study to examine the effect of three treatments, Synectics model(SM), Gaming Strategy(GS) and Traditional Method(TM) of teaching towards creativity and their interaction with sex. The sample comprised of 162 learners of VI grade divided into two, the experimental and control group. The experiment was carried for four months. Intelligence and age of learners was controlled. It was found that the overall creative scores of the learners taught through SM, GM and TM have differential effect upon creativity of boys and girls.

2.8 Conclusions

Educational research in general and research in the field of models of teaching in particular, are of recent origin. It is hopeful sign that research on models of teaching is generally receiving due importance.

It was observed that studies on models of teaching were by and large based on experimental designs. Most of the experiments have been carried out in actual classroom settings and are quasi experimental. Designing such studies in the classroom situation has an advantage of assessing the effectiveness of a teaching strategy in real conditions. It was also observed that creative thinking and ability to solve problems could be enhanced by disciplined procedures like training in creative problem solving, creative writing exercises etc.

There were very few studies conducted on Synectics Model of teaching. Those which were available adopted the model for teaching in the subject of languages like Hindi and English. Though an action research was taken up by Anandi Martis and D'hima(1987) on Synectics model of teaching science, its effect on composite creativity was found. The components of creativity like fluency, flexibility and originality were not studied separately.

There are two strategies of teaching in Synectics model. The first strategy refers to 'making familiar strange'(MFS) and the second strategy refers to 'making strange familiar'(MSF). Most of the studies have adopted the first strategy. The second strategy i.e. the MSF approach has rarely been adopted. One study by Anandi Martis was taken up to develop MSF competencies through Synectics model of teaching in graduate student teachers. It was observed that there is no study on Synectics model of teaching science adopting the MSF approach at secondary school level in Indian settings. It was also observed that development of problem solving ability which is an important side effect of Synectics model of teaching is not at all studied. Hence the present investigation is a modest venture in this direction.

After having discussed the related studies and their implications to the present study the methodology followed in the study is being discussed in the next chapter.

3

Methodology

In the previous chapter literature pertaining to the present study has been discussed. This chapter deals with the procedural details such as the statement of the problem, objectives, variables, operational definitions of terms, statement of hypothesis, design of the study, tools of research, sampling procedure and the conduction of the experiment.

3.1 Statement of the Problem

The problem selected for the present investigation was,

"A STUDY OF EFFECTIVENESS OF SYNECTICS MODEL OF TEACHING SCIENCE ON CREATIVITY AND PROBLEM SOLVING ABILITY OF SECONDARY SCHOOL STUDENTS".

3.2 General Objectives of the Study

The following are the broad objectives of the study

1. Compare the effectiveness of Synectics Model and Conventional Method of teaching science in terms of fostering Fluency, Flexibility and Originality-Components of Creativity and Composite Creativity
2. Compare the effectiveness of Synectics Model and Conventional Method of teaching science in terms of inducing Problem Solving Ability.

3. Investigate interaction between 'treatments' and 'levels of students' with reference to fostering Fluency, Flexibility, Originality-components of Creativity and Composite Creativity

4. Investigate interaction between 'treatments' and 'levels of students' with reference to inducing Problem Solving Ability.

5. Investigate interaction between 'treatments' and 'gender' with reference to fostering Fluency, Flexibility, Originality -components of Creativity and Composite Creativity.

6. Investigate interaction between 'treatments' and 'gender' with reference to inducing Problem Solving Ability.

7. Investigate whether the students sustain Fluency, Flexibility, Originality-components of Creativity and Composite Creativity fostered through Synectics Model of teaching science.

8. Investigate whether the students sustain Problem Solving Ability induced through Synectics Model of teaching science.

3.3 Specific Objectives of the Study

The study was undertaken with the following specific objectives:

1. To compare the effectiveness of Synectics Model and Conventional Method of teaching science in terms of fostering Fluency- a component of Creativity.

2. To compare the effectiveness of Synectics Model and Conventional Method of teaching science in terms of fostering Flexibility - a component of Creativity.

3. To compare the effectiveness of Synectics Model and Conventional Method of teaching science in terms of fostering Originality - a component of Creativity.

4. To compare the effectiveness of Synectics Model and Conventional Method of teaching science in terms of fostering Composite Creativity

5. To compare the effectiveness of Synectics Model and Conventional Method of teaching science in terms of inducing Problem Solving Ability.

6. To investigate interaction between 'treatments' (aforesaid teaching modes) and 'levels of students' (determined on the basis of general mental ability and higher mental ability in science) with reference to fostering Fluency - a components of Creativity.

7. To investigate interaction between 'treatments' and 'levels of students' with reference to fostering Flexibility- a component of Creativity.

8. To investigate interaction between 'treatments' and 'levels of students' with reference to fostering Originality a component of Creativity.

9. To investigate interaction between 'treatments' and 'levels of students' with reference to fostering Composite Creativity

10. To investigate interaction between 'treatments' and 'levels of students' with reference to inducing Problem Solving Ability.

11. To investigate interaction between 'treatments' and 'gender' with reference to fostering Fluency- a component of Creativity.

12. To investigate interaction between 'treatments' and

'gender' with reference to fostering Flexibility - a component of Creativity,

13. To investigate interaction between 'treatments' and 'gender' with reference to fostering Originality- a component of Creativity.

14. To investigate interaction between 'treatments' and 'gender' with reference to fostering Composite Creativity

15. To investigate interaction between 'treatments' and 'gender' with reference to inducing Problem Solving Ability.

16. To investigate whether the students sustain Fluency - a component of Creativity fostered through Synectics Model of teaching science.

17. To investigate whether the students sustain Flexibility - a component of Creativity fostered through Synectics Model of teaching science.

18. To investigate whether the students sustain Originality - a component of Creativity fostered through Synectics Model of teaching science.

19. To investigate whether the students sustain Composite Creativity fostered through Synectics Model of teaching science

20. To investigate whether the students sustain Problem Solving Ability induced through Synectics Model of teaching science.

3.4 Variables of the Study

The variables used in the study are classified into independent, dependent and moderate variables.

(i) Independent Variable

- Treatments viz., (a) Synectics Model of Teaching Science
  (b) Conventional Method of Teaching Science.

(ii) Dependent variables

- Fluency
- Flexibility
- Originality
- Composite Creativity
- Problem Solving Ability.

(iii) Moderate variables

- Levels of students
- gender

3.5 Operational Definitions

A number of terms and concepts have been used in the study. To convey the specific meaning an attempt has been made to explain in what sense these terms and concepts have been used in the present study.

1. Synectics Model

Synectics is an interesting approach to the development of creativity designed by William. J.J. Gordan and his associates. Synectics means joining together of different and apparently irrelevant elements. It is also called cross marriage of ideas.

Synectics Model is an instructional procedure which involves use of analogies. In synectic exercises students play with analogies until they relax and begin to enjoy making more and more metaphoric comparisons. Then they use analogies to attack problems or ideas. It leads the students into a slightly illogical world to give them the opportunity to invent new ways of seeing things, expressing themselves and approaching problems.

2. *Conventional Method*

This method of teaching is text book centered, teacher dominant, examination oriented. The emphasis here is mainly in remembering and reproducing of scientific facts, principles and theories. The students are passive listeners and do not participate actively in the teaching-learning process. This method is by and large being used by secondary school teachers at present.

3. *Creativity*

It is a process where the individual locates gaps in ideas, thinks of alternative solutions to a problem, persists in idea, does not easily agree to what usually is thought to be correct and has unique ways of thinking or doing. Fluency, Flexibility and Originality are the three components of Creativity.

a) Fluency: It is the ability of an individual to produce as many ideas as possible to a given idea where quantity is emphasized than the quality of ideas.

b) Flexibility: It is the ability to produce a great variety of ideas with freedom from preservation.

c) Originality: This component of creativity refers to unusualness of responses or remote associations and relationships of responses. One who tries to get away from the ordinary or conventional is said to have more scope on originality.

4. *Problem Solving Ability*

A 'problem' means a task that can be defined external to

the individual, such as a puzzle, anagram, a maze, or other task in which a observable solution is provided. Problem solving ability is the ability of a person to apply his past experience to arrive at a solution not previously known to the person - atleast in the particular situation presented. In other words it is the ability of an individual to use acquired knowledge, skills and understanding to satisfy the demands of an unfamiliar situation. The individual must synthesize the knowledge and apply it to the new and different situation.

5. *Higher Mental Ability in Science*

It may be defined as the product resulting from application, analysis, synthesis and evaluation of all information concerning to science.

6. *General Mental Ability*

It is the ability of a person to apprehend, observe and conceive relation and develop systematic method of reasoning which indicates his capacity for intellectual activity and clarity in thinking.

7. *Interaction*

It is the differential response to one factor in combination with varying levels of second factor applied simultaneously. In other words, interaction is an additional effect due to the combined influence of two or more factors.

8. *Gender*

It is considered as one of the moderate or intervening variables. In the present study the term 'gender' refers to 'boys and girls' of IX standard of a secondary school.

3.6 Major Hypotheses

The following major hypotheses were formulated in pursuance of the broad objectives of the study:

1. Synectics Model is more effective than the Conventional Method of teaching science in terms of fostering Fluency, Flexibility, Originality and Composite Creativity.
2. Synectics Model is more effective than the Conventional Method of teaching science in terms of inducing Problem Solving Ability.
3. There is interaction between 'treatments' and 'levels' with reference to fostering Fluency, Flexibility, Originality and Composite Creativity.
4. There is interaction between 'treatments' and 'levels' with reference to inducing Problem Solving Ability.
5. There is interaction between 'treatments' and 'gender' with reference to fostering Fluency, Flexibility, Originality and Composite Creativity.
6. There is interaction between 'treatments' and 'gender' with reference to inducing Problem Solving Ability.
7. Immediate and delayed post test scores of the experimental group differ significantly with reference to Fluency, Flexibility, Originality and Composite Creativity.
8. Immediate and delayed post test scores of the experimental group differ significantly with reference to Problem Solving Ability.

3.7 Research Hypotheses

The following research hypotheses were set up in pursuance of the specific objectives of the study:

1. Synectics Model is more effective than the Conventional Method of teaching science in terms of fostering 'Fluency' - a component of Creativity.

2. Synectics Model is more effective than the Conventional Method of teaching science in terms of fostering 'Flexibility' - a component of Creativity.

3. Synectics Model is more effective than the Conventional Method of teaching science in terms of fostering 'Originality' - a component of Creativity.

4. Synectics Model is more effective than the Conventional Method of teaching science in terms of fostering Composite Creativity.

5. Synectics Model is more effective than the Conventional Method of teaching science in terms of inducing Problem Solving Ability.

6. There is interaction between 'treatments' and ' levels' with reference to fostering 'Fluency' - a component of Creativity,

7. There is interaction between 'treatments' and 'levels' with reference to fostering 'Flexibility'—a component of Creativity.

8. There is interaction between 'treatments' and 'levels' with reference to fostering Originality'—a component of Creativity.

9. There is interaction between 'treatments' and 'levels' with reference to fostering Composite Creativity.

10. There is interaction between 'treatments' and 'levels' with reference to inducing Problem Solving Ability.

11. There is interaction between 'treatments' and 'gender' with reference to fostering 'Fluency'—a component of Creativity.

12. There is interaction between 'treatments' and 'gender' with reference to fostering 'Flexibility'—a component of Creativity.

13. There is interaction between 'treatments' and 'gender' with reference to fostering 'Flexibility' - a component of Creativity.
14. There is interaction between 'treatments' and 'gender' with reference to fostering Composite Creativity.
15. There is interaction between 'treatments' and 'gender' with reference to inducing Problem Solving Ability.
16. Immediate and delayed post test scores of the experimental group differ significantly with reference to 'Fluency' - a component of Creativity.
17. Immediate and delayed post test scores of the experimental group differ significantly with reference to 'Flexibility'- a component of Creativity.
18. Immediate and delayed post test scores of the experimental group differ significantly with reference to 'Originality' - a component Creativity.
19. Immediate and delayed post test scores of the experimental group differ significantly with reference to Composite Creativity.
20. Immediate and delayed post test scores of the experimental group differ significantly with reference to Problem Solving Ability.

3.8 Null Hypotheses

For testing the significance of difference, null hypothesis is an useful form of stating hypothesis. Hence, the research hypothesis are stated in the null form below:

1. There is no significant difference between Synectics Model and Conventional Method of teaching science, in terms of fostering 'Fluency' - a component of Creativity,

2. There is no significant difference between Synectics Model and Conventional Method of teaching science in terms of fostering 'Flexibility' - a component of Creativity.
3. There is no significant difference between Synectics Model and Conventional Method of teaching science in terms of fostering 'Originality'- a component of Creativity.
4. There is no significant difference between Synectics Model and Conventional Method of teaching science in terms of fostering Composite Creativity.
5. There is no significant difference between Synectics Model and Conventional Method of teaching science in terms of inducing Problem Solving Ability.
6. There is no interaction between 'treatments' and 'levels' with reference to fostering 'Fluency' - a component of Creativity.
7. There is no interaction between 'treatments' and 'levels' with reference to fostering 'Flexibility' - a component of Creativity.
8. There is no interaction between 'treatments' and 'levels' with reference to fostering 'Originality' - a component of Creativity.
9. There is no interaction between 'treatments' and 'levels' with reference to fostering Composite Creativity.
10. There is no interaction between 'treatments' and 'levels' with reference to inducing Problem Solving Ability.
11. There is no interaction between 'treatments' and 'gender' with reference to fostering Fluency- a component of Creativity.

12. There is no interaction between 'treatments' and 'gender' with reference to fostering Flexibility-a component of Creativity.
13. There is no interaction between 'treatments' and 'gender' with reference to fostering Originality-a component of Creativity.
14. There is no interaction between 'treatments' and 'gender' with reference to fostering Composite Creativity.
15. There is no interaction between 'treatments' and 'gender' with reference to inducing Problem Solving Ability.
16. Immediate and delayed post test scores of the experimental group do not differ significantly with reference to 'Fluency'-a component of Creativity.
17. Immediate and delayed post test scores of experimental group do not differ significantly with reference to 'Flexibility' -a component of Creativity.
18. Immediate and delayed post test scores of experimental group do not differ significantly with reference to 'Originality' - a component of Creativity.
19. Immediate and delayed post test scores of experimental group do not differ significantly with reference to Composite Creativity.
20. Immediate and delayed post test scores of experimental group do not differ significantly with reference to Problem Solving Ability.

3.9 Design of the Experiment

The study was experimental in nature. Pre-test post-test parallel group (TXL) experimental design was followed in the present study. TXL design was found to be most appropriate after review of literature in experimental designs.

In this design inter subject variations could be directly controlled and the treatments are administered to samples that have been matched with reference to a control variable. This design also permits a separate study of effect of treatment at different levels of control variable. Moreover this design provides for direct control of Type 's' errors. Hence keeping the above facts in view, the TXL was selected for the present study. The TXL design as applied to the study is diagrammatically represented in figure3.1

		Levels		
		L_1 (Above Average)	L_2 (Average)	L_3 (Below Average)
Treatment	Synectics Model (T_1)	n T_1 L_1	n T_1 L_2	n T_1 L_3
	Conventional Method (T_2)	n T_2 L_1	n T_2 L_2	n T_2 L_3

Fig 3.1 Diagrammatic representation of Treatments and levels.

3.10 Selection or Construction of Tools

In experimental studies, two kinds of information are needed. Firstly, the nature of the sample and secondly, the measurement of desirable behavioural changes in the sample as a result of treatment variables. For collecting this information good instruments are required and the researcher looks for the best available tools.

In the present study two tests viz.;

(i) Standard Programme Matrices (SPM)

(ii) Test of Higher Mental Ability in Science (THMAS)

were used to obtain two matched groups. As a result of treatment variables there would be some change in the dependent variables. For measuring these changes the following two tests were used;

(i) Verbal Test of Creative Thinking (VTCT) and

(ii) Problem Solving Ability Test (PSAT)

Among the tests used for measuring the dependent variables, the second one i.e. PSAT was constructed by the researcher herself. The other tests used were standardised tests. The details in respect of tools used are given in the following paragraphs.

3.10.1 Standard Progressive Matrices (SPM)

Raven (1938) developed a nonverbal culture free test by name progressive matrices, to measure the intelligence of literate as well as illiterate individuals. It tests a person's capacity to apprehend meaningless figures presented for his observation. He sees the relationship between them, conceives the nature of figures completing each system of relations presented and develop a systematic method of reasoning. The test provides an opportunity for the assessment of a person's capacity for intellectual activity. This test was designed to be used with persons of all ages, whatever their education, nationality and physical condition.

Standard Progressive Matrices consists of five sets of items (A,B,C,D&E). Each set has 12 items, constituting 60 items in all in the test. Each item has a large design in which a portion is missing. Below each item six alternative answers with numbers are given. The candidate is required to identify the correct answer and record it in a separate answer sheet provided for this purpose. The answers can be scored with the help of the scoring key given in the manual.

(a) Reliability

(i) Test- retest reliabilities reported by the authors Stinissen, Dolke, Sheppard & Goetzinger) range from 0.80 to 0.93.

(ii) Consistency reliabilities reported, range from 0.87 to

0.97 (Blansk & Sinha, Elley & Mac Arthur King, Laroche & Bruke).

(b) Validity

(i) Concurrent validity: The corelations of SPM with Binet & Wescheler scale range from 0.54 to 0.86 ·

(ii) Predictive validities of SPM with scholastic achievement range up to 0.70.

(iii) Factoral Validity - The progressive matrices has been described as one of the purest and best of the available measures of general intellectual functioning ('g'). Factor analytic studies reveal high loading up to 0.83 on 'g'.

3.10.2 Test of Higher Mental Ability in Science (THMAS)

Sansanwal & Anuradha Joshi developed and standardised this test in 1989. It assesses the higher mental abilities like application, analysis, synthesis and evaluation in relation to science. The test contains 20 items and covers the above four abilities with 6,6,5 & 3 items each respectively. Some are open ended and some are multiple choice questions. Though the items make use of science content, they are coined in such a way that they assess the above said abilities and not knowledge or comprehension of science content. There is no time limit for the completion of the test and it can be used for the age group of 14 -17 years and also at the + 2 stage.

(a) Reliability: The test - retest reliability is reported to range from 0.514 to 0.816 (n =110)

(b) Validity: The concurrent validity of the test with science achievement & total academic achievement are found to be 0.24 (n=104) and 0.26 (n=102) respectively.

3.10.3 Verbal Test of Creative Thinking (VTCT)

Baqer Mehdi has developed and standardised this test

of creative thinking in 1973. This test could be used to identify creative talent of children of all stages of education except for pre-primary & primary stages. It consists of two subtests. (i) Verbal test of creative thinking and (ii) Non-verbal test of creativity thinking. These subtests include tasks pertaining to four traits (as enumerated by Guilford) viz., Fluency, Flexibility, Originality & Elaboration. These four traits used in the tests are considered to give fairly valid measure of creative potential of the individual. The verbal test of creative thinking includes four sub-tests viz., Consequences test, Unusual uses test, New relationships test and Product improvement test.

a) Consequences Test: This test consists of three hypothetical situation and the pupil is required to think of as many novel, interesting and unusual uses of these objects he can think of. The time allowed for each task is five minutes.

b) Unusual uses Test : This test presents the names of three common objects and pupil is required to write as many novel, interesting and unusual uses of these objects he can think of. The time allowed for each task is five minutes.

c) New relationships Test: This test presents three pairs of words apparently different and the pupil is required to think of as many novel relationships between the two objects of each pair. The test provides an opportunity for free play of imagination & originality. The time given for each pair of words is five minutes.

d) Product Improvement Test: In this test the pupil requires to think of a simple wooden toy of a horse and suggest additions of new things to make it more interesting for children to play with. The time limit is six minutes.

SCORING:

Scoring can be done with the help of the scoring sheet given in the manual.

Reliability of the Test:

The test - retest reliabilities of the factor scores and also the total score were obtained on a sample (N = 31). This is shown in Table-3.1

Table 3.1 Test-retest reliabilities for factor scores and the total Creativity score for N=31 as reported by the author, Baqer Mehdi, 1977.

Fluency	Flexibility	Originality	Total Creativity
0.945	0.921	0.896	0.929

Validity:

Concurrent validity coefficients against teacher ratings for each factor is given in table 3.2 below. The sample considered was 300.

Table 3.2 : Concurrent validity coefficients against teacher ratings for each factor (N=300)

Fluency	Flexibility	Originality	Total Creativity
0.40	0.32	0.34	0.39

The other part of the test i.e. Non-Verbal Test of Creative Thinking was not used in the present study to assess creative thinking ability of students, since the Synectics Model promotes verbal expressiveness.

3.10.4 Problem Solving Ability Test(PSAT)

Tests of problem solving ability should really measure an individual's ability to solve problems. These tests should be different from achievement tests that are content loaded. So before a tool is accepted for this purpose, one should remember that (i) it is different from conventional achievement test, hence the items of the test should be content free (ii) must show that pupils acquiring high scores on these tests are capable of solving problems and follow the steps of a researcher in finding out solutions to their problems.

3.10.4.1 Need for Developing this Test

Several attempts have been made to develop paper pencil tests meant to be administered in group situations for measuring problem solving ability. Most of the attempts made include content items in their tests. Problem solving ability tests in mathematics include content from mathematics and problem solving ability tests in science include problems which are based on science content.

Some tests are developed in foreign countries. But very few researches are reported in India. Some researches attempted to construct test including multiple choice items and mazes. But they mostly appear to be science achievement tests i.e. it needs the students to have knowledge in science and first aid facts to select the answer. Thus by referring to the related literature and studies involving construction of tests measuring problem solving ability, the following observations could be made

(i) Although tests measuring problem solving ability are available, few tests suit Indian conditions.

(ii) Although a few tests developed in Indian researches are available, some include multiple choice items and do not consider the steps involved in the problem solving procedure. The others have items based on content in science and mathematics.

(iii) The few available tests developed by Indian researchers do not suit the present study.

On the basis of these observations the researcher decided to develop a content free test measuring problem solving ability with due emphasis on the steps involved in the problem solving process. Although a few items need some knowledge of science, it is very general and basic and do not need high technical knowledge.

The following are the major steps of problem solving included for measurement.

(i) Definition of the problem.

(ii) Clues identified to arrive at a solution.

(iii) The final solution arrived at.

(i) Definition of the problem: The students clearly understand, present and clearly define the problem.

(ii) Clues identified to arrive at a solution: The students identify and assemble the significant related facts and pertinent information. They also recall previously acquired information which might be helpful towards the solution of the problem.

(iii) The final solution arrived at: The students identify and examine possible conclusions which might be drawn from the collected data. They consider ways in which the problem might be solved by keeping the information gathered and evaluated. Thus they attempt to reach at logical and reasonable decisions or solutions.

3.10.4.2 Drafting the Test

Based on the above steps of problem solving the test was developed using the scientific procedure , collecting, writing and screening of items. Thirty three divergent problems, mystery plots and consequences situations were prepared. The following criteria were used for selecting or writing the items:

(i) Solving of divergent problems:

a) Framing of the creative problem-Is it interesting?

b) Does the problem lend itself for divergent solutions?

c) Are all the conditions necessary for solving the problem given?

d) Variety of problems.

(ii) Solving of mystery plots:

a) Are the problems such that the students really feel it to be a mystery?

b) Variety of plots.

c) Is clue to solve the problem hidden in it?

(iii) Consequence situations:

a) Do the problem have elements of imagination?

b) Variety

c) Is it very general and does not require high technical knowledge?

The vocabulary and the language structure for the level of ninth standard children were also kept as a criteria for selecting and preparing the items. The problems included in the draft test is given in Appendix-A (I). The items indicating problem situations thus prepared were subject to scrutiny by ten experts and the guide. They have examined the items and unanimously agreed that all the items pooled are competent to assess the ability of students to solve problems. The experts offered a few candid suggestions to refine the items. It was also suggested to give an example in the beginning to demonstrate the way in which the students ought to give the responses. It was also suggested to decrease the length of the test and to select ten to fifteen items from the total thirty three items of the draft test.

3.10.4.3 Scoring

Simple scoring method was followed for giving weightage to the responses of the students. One mark each was awarded to the first and second step correctly answered. The third and the final step i.e. arriving at the final solution is awarded with one mark for every relevant, possible, unrepeated solution. The students are strictly instructed to write all the steps. However, if the student has written relevant, possible solution without attempting to write the first two steps then the marks allotted for these two steps are also awarded as it is reasoned out that if the student is able to suggest a relevant, possible solution to a situation, then he must have gone through the first two steps. In other words the score that the student can get in this test was ranged from zero and above.

3.10.4.4 Pilot study

A pilot study was conducted on fifty secondary school students of ninth standard. The scores collected from this pilot study were subjected to item analysis.

3.10.4.5 Item Analysis

All the thirty three items were evaluated by computing the difficulty index and the discriminatory power. After finding out the item difficulty and discriminatory power of the items, fifteen items which had acceptable difficulty index and discriminatory power were selected from the thirty three items after the try out for the final tool. Table 3.1 shows the difficulty index and the discriminatory power of the selected fifteen items.

The selected fifteen items were arranged in ascending order of their index of difficulty. In the beginning an easy item was included to encourage the students to continue with the test.

Table 3.1: Difficulty index and Discriminatory power of the selected fifteen items of PSAT

Item No.	Difficulty Index	Index of Discriminatory power
1	0.35	0.69
2	0.39	0.77
3	0.42	0.69
4	0.53	0.92
5	0.54	0.62
6	0.54	0.31
7	0.54	0.77
8	0.58	0.39
9	0.62	0.46
10	0.62	0.62
11	0.65	0.63
12	0.65	0.54
13	0.69	0.46
14	0.69	0.46
15	0.8	0.39

3.10.4.6 Item Validity

Item validity was computed to the fifteen items selected based on difficulty index and discriminatory power. Tetrachoric correlation technique was employed to find out item validities. The item validities of the test is shown in Table 3.2.

Since the obtained validity coefficients of all the items are positive and, are highly or moderately significant, the fifteen items have been retained in the test.

Table 3.2 Item validities for the selected fifteen items of PSAT

(n = 50)

Item No.	Tetrachoric correlation Coefficient-rt	Significance
1	0.54	Yes
2	0.54	Yes
3	0.3	Yes
4	0.3	Yes
5	0.42	Yes
6	0.65	Yes
7	0.58	Yes
8	0.79	Yes
9	0.58	Yes
10	0.88	Yes
11	0.7	Yes
12	0.64	Yes
13	0.89	Yes
14	0.86	Yes
15	1.00	Yes

3.10.4.7 Reliability of the test

(i) Test-retest reliability : Retest was conducted on students after a gap of 30 days from the first administration. Test-retest reliability was computed using Pearson's product moment correlation. The computation of Pearson's product moment correlation is given in Appendix A (III -a). The obtained correlation coefficient was found to be 0.75, which is highly significant.

(ii) Split-half reliability : Stanley's formula for finding split half reliability by the split half method was used. The formula is as given below :

$$r = 1 - \frac{D_d^2}{D_s^2}$$

where D_d^2 → squared difference between the sum of difference scores on the 27% of papers having largest half test difference score and the sum of difference scores on the lower 27%.

D_s^2 → squared difference between the sum of total scores on the 27% of papers having higher total scores and the sum of total scores on 27% of papers having smallest total scores.

The detailed procedure of calculation is given in Appendix D(III - b).

Substituting in the formula

$$r = 1 - \frac{D_d^2}{D_s^2}$$

$$r = 1 - \frac{[72-(-67)]^2}{(791-310)^2}$$

$$r = 1 - \frac{19321}{231361}$$

$$r = 1 - 0.08$$

$$r = 0.92$$

The obtained reliability coefficient i.e. r = 0.92 was found to be highly significant.

3.10.4.8 Validity of the test

The opinion of experts was taken for examining the content validity and construct validity of the test. For concurrent validity the ratings of the teachers regarding the problem solving ability of the students were considered . Two teachers, one who teaches mathematics and the other who teaches science were briefed about the present investigation and oriented about the nature of the problem solving and characteristics of a good problem solver. They were requested to rate these students, independent of each other on a two point scale as Good Problem Solver(GPS) and Poor Problem Solver(PPS). Most of the ratings of pupils given by the two teachers were in agreement with each other. Only those which were in agreement with each other were retained for finding the validity.

The teacher's ratings and total problem solving ability scores were taken and Tetrachoric correlation coefficient was computed between them. Teachers ratings and the respective scores are given in Appendix A (IV). The computation of Tetrachoric correlation coefficient is shown below

		Teacher's Ratings		
		GP	PP	
PSAT scores	AM	6^{B}	15^{A}	21
	BM	23^{D}	1^{C}	24
		29	16	45

$$rt = \cos\frac{180\sqrt{BC}}{\sqrt{AD}+\sqrt{BC}}$$

$$rt = \cos\frac{180\sqrt{(6)(1)}}{\sqrt{(15)(23)}+\sqrt{(6)(1)}}$$

$$rt = \cos\frac{441}{21.02}$$

$$rt = \cos 20.98$$

$$rt = 0.93$$

There is a high significant correlation between teachers ratings and total problem solving ability scores. Thus it could be concluded that the test has concurrent validity.

3.11 Sampling Procedure

Multistage purposive sampling technique was followed. The procedure of selection of the sample is as follows:

3.11.1 Selection of School

A suitable school where the experiment could be conducted was identified. The investigator selected Florence High School located in Bangalore City keeping the following facts in view.

(i) The willing cooperation of the head of the institution and members of the staff.

(ii) The strength of students in the class for size of the sample was to be between thirty and forty.

(iii) Regularity of students attending the class.

(iv) Co-education school, as the sample needed both boys and girls.

The experiment was conducted in a single school so that the extraneous variables could be controlled. The extraneous variables might come into play due to the inter-school differences in the school atmosphere.

3.11.2 Selection of Class

The experimental treatment involves the use of Synectics

model. The students who are to be taught by Synectics approach need to participate actively through verbal expressions. The students are required to have fair amount of vocabulary for suggesting, playing and making comparisons with analogies as per the model. For eighth grade the researcher could not be sure that the students would have this minimal ability as they come from different primary schools. The school authorities were not ready to spare tenth grade. Moreover the researcher did not find tenth grade as an appropriate class since S.S.L.C. examination serves as a turning point to their future, as such students will be looking for better performance. Therefore students participation in the experiment would not be to the expected level.

The ninth grade students are under the age group of 14-15 years would have transited into formal operational stage. As per Piaget, the children under formal operational stage would be capable of hypothetical and propositional thoughts, reflective thinking, abstract conceptual and logical thinking and other mental tasks. As the study intends to investigate into the effect of Synectics Model on development of Problem Solving Ability the students of IX standard were found appropriate to be selected as the sample of the study. Hence ninth grade was considered to be the suitable class both from academic and administrative points of view of conducting the experiment.

3.11.3 Obtaining Two Parallel Groups

The staff members of the school were consulted by the investigator for selection of two sections of ninth grade, as there were four sections (A,B, C and D). The staff members suggested 'B' and 'C' sections as the students in these two classes were active and enthusiastic in their opinion and were almost parallel in respect to achievement and interest in studies.

Ninth 'B' and Ninth 'C' had a student strength of 54 and

53 respectively. Both the sections had to be matched on intellectual capacity and higher mental ability in science. Hence fifty students of each division were administered, Standard Progressive Matrices(SPM) and Test of Higher Mental Ability in Science(THMAS). Product-moment correlation coefficient was computed to find out the index of relationship between these two set of scores. The obtained coefficient of correlation was positive. This suggested that matching could be done on both the variables. Hence both the scores were clubbed for the purpose of matching to get matched pairs. For this raw scores on both the tests were converted into T-scores by using the formula .

$$T = 10Z + 50$$

Where $$Z = \frac{X - \overline{X}}{SD}$$

$$T = \frac{10(X - \overline{X})}{SD} + 50$$

The obtained T scores on both these test were added to get a Composite T-score on SPM and THMAS taken together as in Appendix B(I) and B(II). Exactly or most nearly matching pairs of students were identified by arranging the scores in descending order classwise. Thus thirty matched pairs of students were obtained [Appendix B(III)]. This formed the sample of the study.

Out of these two divisions the experimental and control groups were selected, by choosing a chit and random decision was made. Thirty students of ninth 'B' formed the experimental group and thirty students of ninth 'C' formed the control group. The sampling procedure is diagrammatically shown in Figure 3.2.

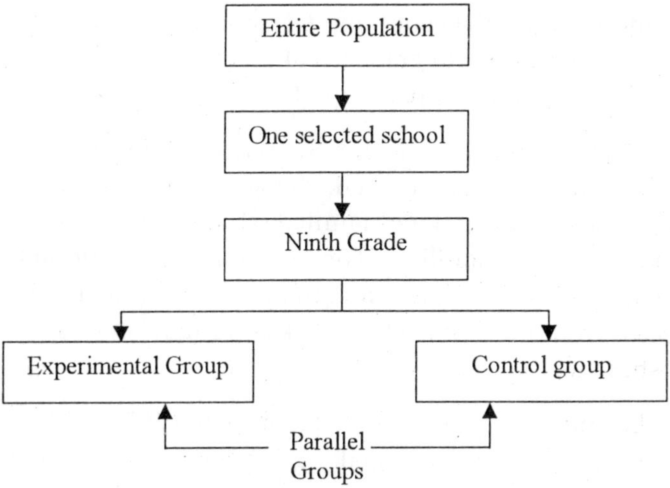

Fig 3.2 Diagrammatic representation of sampling procedure.

3.12 Constitution of Levels

The experimental design needed three levels of students from the sample. So the composite T-scores on SPM and THMAS of each group were arranged in descending order. The 'top one third' of the cases of each group were treated as 'above average level' of students (L1). The 'bottom one third' formed the 'below average level' of students (L3) and the 'middle one third' of the cases were treated as 'average level' of students (L2).

3.13 Preparations for Conducting the Experiment

The researcher thoroughly studied the theory behind model of teaching in general and Synectics Model in particular. Some related studies conducted in the area were also reviewed and the format of the lessons were studied and discussed with few experts.

After acquaintance with the theoretical background of Synectics model, the researcher has identified twenty five topics of ninth grade science syllabus which have wider scope for adoption of Synectics model of teaching. The topics selected from the ninth grade syllabus for adopting Synectics model are given in Appendix C(I)

A lesson plan guide for Synectics model of teaching science was also developed. Synectics model has two approaches, one 'making familiar strange' and the other 'making strange familiar'. The researcher has selected the second approach i.e. 'making strange familiar' as the topics selected from the science text book were new and strange to the students.

Lesson plans for the selected topics were written following the lesson plan guide for 'making strange familiar' approach of Synectics model of teaching. The lesson plan guide of MSF approach - Syntax II is given in appendix C(II). These lesson plans were placed before a panel of researchers, guide and an expert for scrutiny. The panel also suggested to give one or two trial lessons. Three trial lessons were given by the researcher in ninth grade of another school. The experience gave the researcher an overview of the approach and how the lessons could actually be conducted. The suggestions made by the panel were incorporated and the final set of lesson plans were developed. Three sample lesson plans one each in Physics, Chemistry and Biology are given in Appendix C(III).

3.14 Conduction of the Experiment

The present study is pre-test, post-test parallel group design. In this design the effects of the treatments are judged by the difference between the pre-test and post-test scores. This is compared with the control group.

The main steps involved in the study were:

(i) Experimental and control group were pre-tested on creativity test and problem solving ability test.

(ii) Experimental group was taught by Synectics model

and the control group was taught by the conventional method for a period of two months.

(iii) Both the groups were immediately post tested on creativity test and problem solving ability test.

(iv) The experimental group was delayedely post tested after a gap of six weeks on creativity test and problem solving ability test to see whether they sustain the improvements on dependent variables (creativity and problem solving ability) if any.

The procedure followed in the conduct of the experiment is schematically shown in figure 3.3.

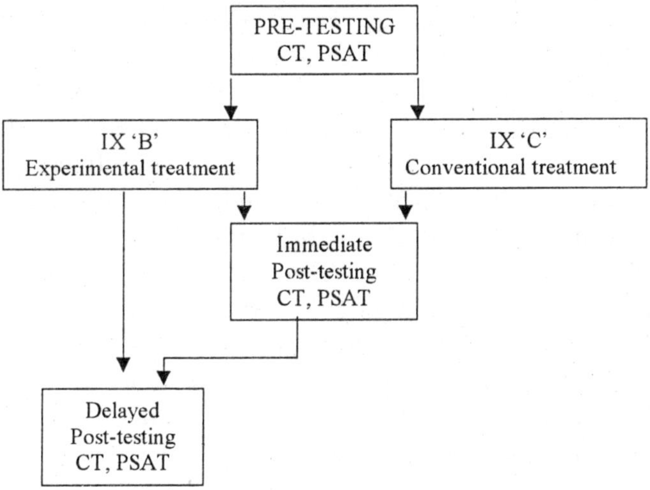

Fig 3.3 Schematic representation of the experimental design.

Pre-testing

The 30 pair of students of both the experimental and control groups were simultaneously pre-tested on Verbal Test of Creative Thinking and Problem Solving Ability Test. One test was conducted each day for both the groups to avoid fatigue.

Applying treatments

The treatment was applied for a period of two months. The Synectics model lessons were given by the researcher on every alternative day i.e. Monday, Wednesday and Friday. The duration of each lesson was forty five minutes. Thus twenty five lessons were taken during the period of two months. Use of analogies and playing with them is an important step in Synectics Model of teaching. Therefore before starting the treatments i.e. actual lessons using Synectics Model of teaching the researcher took ten classes for stretching exercises. During these sessions the students were taught about analogies and types of analogies i.e. personal analogy and direct analogy. The students practiced to give personal analogy for first five sessions and during the next five sessions they exercised the direct analogies. A sample each for stretching exercises in personal analogy and direct analogy are given in Appendix C(IV -a) and C(IV -b) respectively. After this the actual treatment was started. The students were formed into six groups of five students each. Each group was provided with worksheets for Synectics Lessons. A sample of worksheet of a group of students is given in Appendix C(V). Meanwhile, the control group was taught by their regular teacher by using Conventional Method of teaching. This method was teacher dominant, examination oriented, text book centered where the pupil were passive listeners in the classroom.

Immediate post-testing

Immediately after the completion of treatments both the experimental and control group were post-tested on Verbal Test of Creativity and Problem Solving Ability Test.

Delayed post-testing

After the post-test was administered a gap of six weeks was given. After these six weeks the experimental group was post-tested again on the same tools viz., Verbal Test of Creativity and Problem Solving Ability Test, to know the retention of the experimental group of students on these dependent variables.

3.15 Statistical Techniques Used

The pre-test, immediate post-test and delayed post-test answer sheets obtained from the students of both experimental and control groups were scored as per the guidelines and scoring keys of each test. These obtained scores were tabulated and the gain in scores between pre-test and post-test were computed. These gain scores were considered as raw scores for further statistical analysis.

The following statistical techniques were used to analyse the collected data with a view to test the hypotheses.

(i) Two-way Analysis of variance

(ii) 't'-test

(i) Two-way Analysis of Variance : The principle involved in the analysis of variance is the comparison of variability between the various groups with the sum of variability found within the groups. As two-way analysis of variance permits the simultaneous study of two factors as well as interaction between the two, this technique was used for the purpose of analysis of data. The outline of steps followed in computing two-way ANOVA is given in Chapter IV i.e. 'Analysis of Data and Interpretation'.

(ii) t-test: t-test was used to know whether the experimental and control groups differ on the dependent variables initially i.e. before applying the treatments. It was also used to know whether the immediate post-test and delayed post-test scores differ significantly with reference to dependent variables.

3.16 Limitations of the Study

The study has the following limitations

- The study was confined to English medium students only.
- The study was confined to the teaching of science only.
- The study was confined to the thirty students of ninth grade of a school in Bangalore city.
- The study was limited to certain selected topics of ninth grade science syllabus
- Only 'making the strange familiar' approach was followed in the present study.
- The study was limited to finding out the effectiveness of Synectics model on Creativity and Problem solving ability of secondary school students only.

4

Analysis of Data and Interpretation

In the previous chapter the methodology of the study was presented. This includes the operational definitions, discussion of variables, the experimental design, selection and construction of tools the sampling procedure and design of the experiment.

The present chapter aims at presenting the analysis of data collected from the experiment and interpretation of the results. This is given under four sections. Section-1 deals with the data pertaining to confirmation of whether experimental and control group are similar initially with reference to dependent variables in the study. Section-2 deals with analysis of data pertaining to the dependent variable - Creativity. Section-3 deals with the analysis of data relating to the dependent variable- Problem Solving Ability. Section-4 deals with the analysis of data pertaining to sustainity of treatment effects.

For obtaining the raw scores for statistical analysis, the following procedure was followed. The pre-test and post-test scores of every student in the experimental and control groups were tabulated. Then the gain scores i.e. the difference between post-test and pre-test scores of each student in both groups were computed dependent variable wise. These gain scores were considered as raw scores for further statistical analysis.

SECTION - 1

4.1 Comparison of Pre-Test Data of Experimental and Control Groups

The pre-test scores of experimental and control groups, variable wise was compared by applying t-test. This was done to find whether the two groups of students were similar in terms of the dependent variables before subjected to treatments. Though the experimental and control groups were matched on general mental ability and higher mental ability in science this was done to confirm whether there exists any difference between these two groups in terms of the dependent variables - Creativity and Problem Solving Ability. The scores related to comparison of pre-test scores of experimental and control groups with regard to fluency- a component of creativity is shown in table 4.1. The following formula was used for computing t .

$$t = \frac{\Sigma d}{\sqrt{\frac{n\Sigma d^2 - (\Sigma d)^2}{n-1}}} \quad \text{with } df(n-1)$$

The results of the above analysis with reference to the dependent variables are given in the summary of Table 4.2.

Table 4.1 Summary Table of obtained `t' value and their significance with reference to all the dependent variables before treatments.

n = 30 matchedpairs

Sl. No.	Dependent Variable	Obtained 't' value	Tabled 't' value	Significance at 0.05 level
1.	Fluency-component of creativity	-1.71	2.04	NS*
2.	Flexibility-component of creativity	-0.93	2.04	NS*
3.	Originality-component of creativity	-1.59	2.04	NS*
4.	Composite creativity	-1.82	2.04	NS*
5.	Problem Solving Ability	0.27	2.04	NS*

NS* = Not significant

Since the obtained t value (-1.71) is less than the tabled 't' value (2.04) with df 29 at 0.05 level, the difference is not significant. Hence, the null hypothesis stating that 'There is no significant difference between experimental and control group with reference to Fluency - a component of creativity, before treatments', is accepted. This means that both the groups donot differ significantly with respect to fluency. Hence, it may be concluded that both the groups were alike with regard to Fluency - a component of creativity before subjected to the treatments. Similarly Table 4.1 shows that all the obtained 't' values are lesser than the table t-value and the difference is not signifcant. Therefore the null hypotheses stating that 'the experimental and control groups do not differ significantly with reference to the variables considered in the study' are accepted.

From the above findings it may be concluded that experimental and control group students are alike with reference to all the dependent variables before subjected to treatments. This necessary implies that the entry behaviour is the same with reference to the dependent variables. Further it also suggests that matching of the groups was appropriate.

Hence it may be concluded that the difference noticed in creativity and problem solving ability after the application of treatments may be attributed to the treatments alone.

SECTION -2

4.2 Analysis of Data Pertaining to Creativity

The scores on creativity were obtained from three of its components separately viz., Fluency, Flexibility and Originality. Hence analysis is been made separately in part A,B and C. Later the scores on all the three components are summed up and the analysis is made for composite creativity in part D.

Part A

4.2.1 Analysis Pertaining to Fluency - A Component of Creativity

In pursuance of the objectives 1, 6 and 11 i.e, to find if there is significant difference between Synectics Model and Conventional Method of teaching science, in terms of fostering Fluency - a component of Creativity and if there is any interaction between 'treatments' & 'levels' and 'treatments' & 'gender' with reference to fostering Fluency - a component of Creativity, two-way analysis of variance was used. The gain scores of experimental and control groups were compared according to levels with reference to fluency. Summary table of ANOVA according to levels with reference to fluency is given in table 4.2.

Table4.2 Summary table of ANOVA of Fluency by levels and treatments.

Source of Variation	df	SS	MS=SS/df	F	Significance
Levels (A)	3 - 1	441.6	220.8	11.46*	Yes
Treatments (B)	2 - 1	5920.2	5920.2	307.38*	Yes
Interaction (AB)	(3-1)(2-1)	143.5	71.75	3.73+	Yes
Within Groups (Error)	60 - (3)(2)	1039.8	19.26		

* ⇒ Significant at 0.01 level
\+ ⇒ Significant at 0.05 level

(i) The obtained F-value with reference to factor-B treatments is 307.38 and the corresponding tabled value is 7.17 with df, 1 & 54 at 0.01 level. Since the obtained F-value is greater than the tabled value, it is significant. Therefore the corresponding null hypothesis stating that there is no significant difference between Synectics model and conventional method of teaching science with reference to fostering fluency is rejected. Hence, it may be concluded that there is a significant difference between Synectics model and conventional method of teaching science with reference to fostering of fluency.

Since the mean value of gain in fluency scores of experimental group are greater than that of the control group it may be interpreted that Synectics model of teaching science is more effective in fostering fluency when compared to conventional method of teaching science.

(ii) The obtained F-value with reference to interaction is 3.73 which is greater than the corresponding tabled value 3.18 with df 2 & 54 at 0.05 level. Therefore, it may be concluded that the interaction between 'treatments' and 'levels' of students with reference to fostering of fluency is significant.

In other words, when treatments and levels of students are allowed to interact, they are significantly effective. This signifies that, treatments differ in their effectiveness in fostering Fluency depending upon student's levels.

Graph A

In this graph above average and average students of experimental and control groups are compared with regard to 'Fluency' - a component of creativity.

The graph indicates the following interpretations.

1. There is a significant ordinal interaction in which the lines of the graph donot cross. This implies that the improvement of both the above average and average students is in the same direction.

2. The performance of above average students is better than the average students in both the experimental and control groups. But the performance of experimental group is better than that of the control

Graph A
Comparison of Above Average and Average Students of 'E' & 'C' Groups W.R.T. Fluency

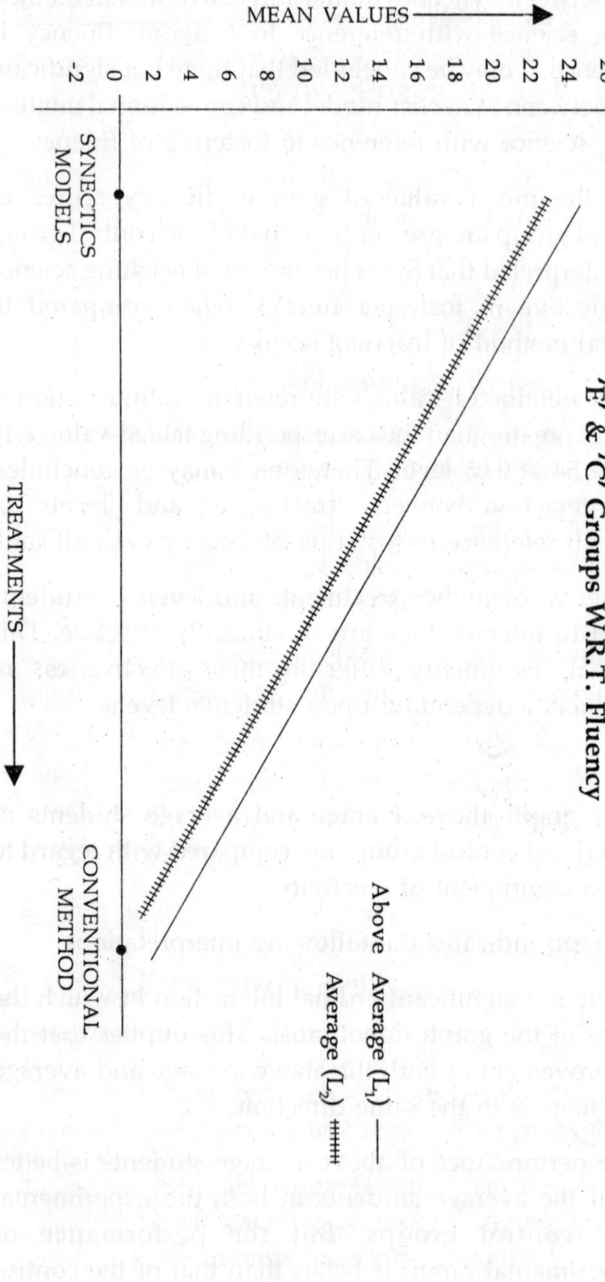

group. In other words, above average students who have undergone treatment in Synectics model have out performed the average students who have undergone treatment in conventional method.

3. The difference in the performance of above average and average students who have undergone treatment in Synectics model is greater when compared to difference in the performance of above average and average students who have undergone treatment in conventional method

Graph B

This graph indicates the comparison of average and below average students of experimental and control groups with regard to the dependent variable, 'Fluency' - a component of creativity.

The graph indicates the following interpretations

1. There is a significant ordinal interaction in which the lines of the graph donot cross. This implies that the improvement of both the average and below average is in the same direction.
2. The performance of average is better than the below average students in both the experimental and control groups. But the performance of experimental group is better than that of the control group. In other words, average students who have undergone treatment in Synectics model have out performed the below average students who have undergone treatment in conventional method.
3. The difference in the performance of average and below average students who have undergone treatment in Synectics Model is greater when compared to difference in the performance of average and below

Graph B
Comparison of Average and Below Average Students of 'E' & 'C' Groups W.R.T. Fluency

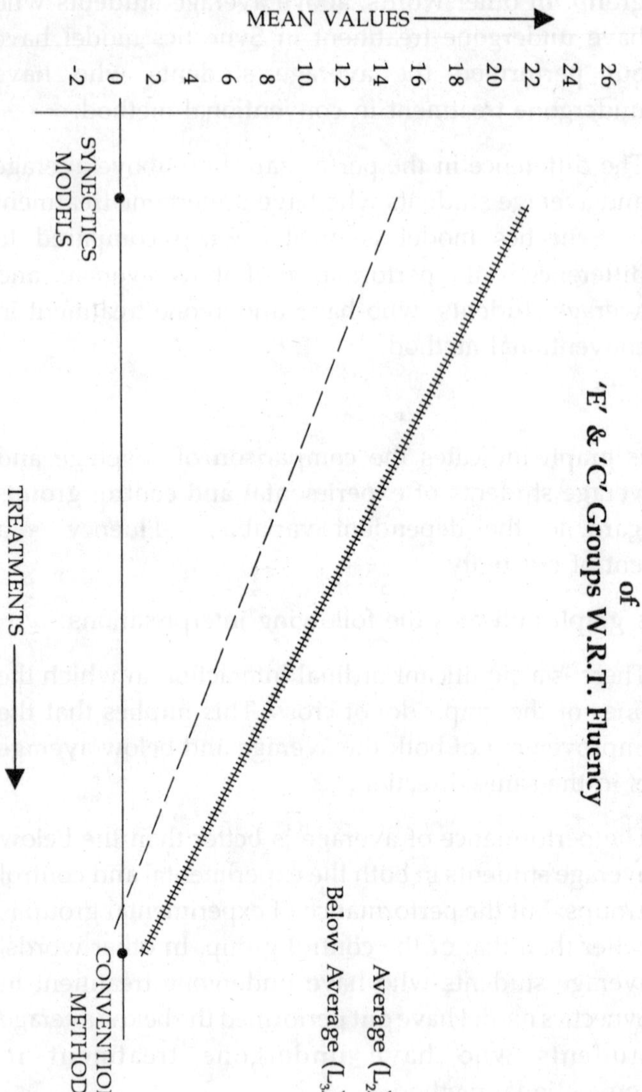

average students who have undergone treatment in conventional method.

Graph C

This graph indicates the comparison of above average and below average students of experimental and control groups with regard to the dependent variable, 'Fluency' - a component of creativity.

The following interpretations can be made from the graph.

1. It indicates a significant ordinal interaction in which the lines of the graph donot cross. This implies that the improvement of both the above average and below average students is in the same direction.
2. The performance of above average is better than the below average students in both the experimental and control groups. But the performance of experimental group is better than that of the control group. In other words, above average students who have undergone treatment in Synectics model have out performed the below average students who have undergone treatment in conventional method.
3. The difference in the performance of above average and below average students who have undergone treatment in Synectics Model is greater when compared to difference in the performance of above average and below average students who have undergone treatment in conventional method.

Graph D

This graph indicates the comparison of above average, average and below average students of experimental and control groups with regard to 'Fluency' - a component of creativity.

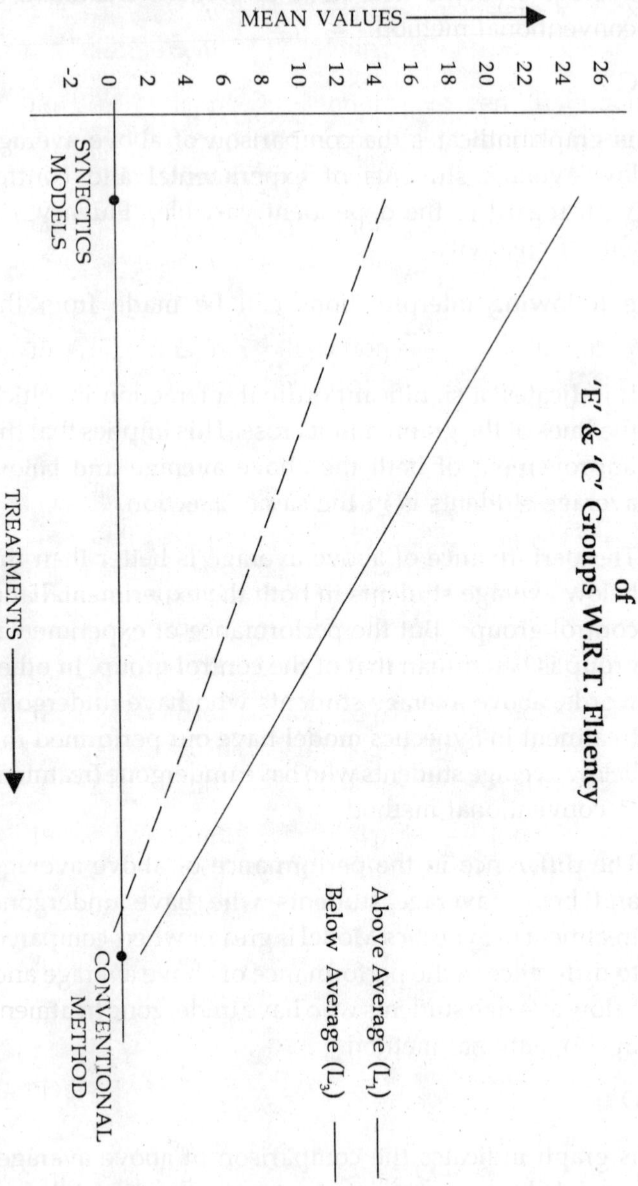

Graph C
Comparison of Above Average and Below Average Students of 'E' & 'C' Groups W.R.T. Fluency

Graph D

Comparison of Above Average, Average and Below Average Students of 'E' & 'C' Groups W.R.T. Fluency

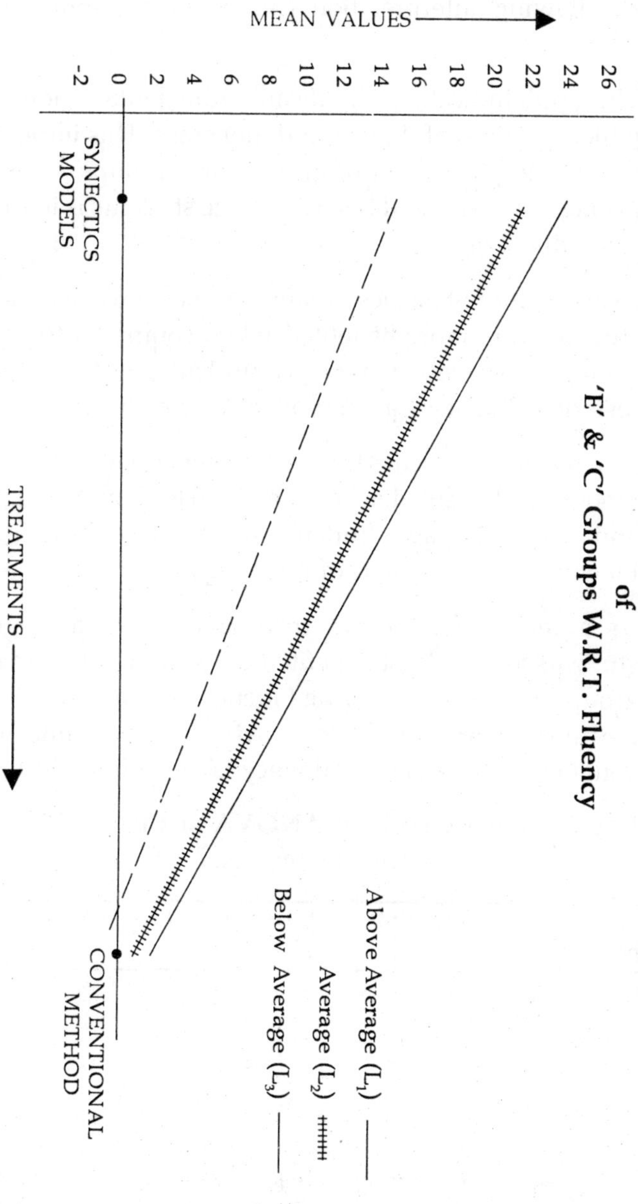

The following interpretation can be made from this graph:

1. The graph indicates a significant ordinal interaction in which the lines of the graph donot cross. This implies that the improvement of all the three groups, above average, average and below average students is in the same direction.

2. As a result of Synectics treatment, the above average students are more benefited when compared to the average and below average students in terms of fostering Fluency - a component of creativity.

3. As a result of Synectics treatment, average students are moderately benefited, when compared to above average and below average students in terms of fostering Fluency - a component of creativity.

4. As a result of Synectics treatment, below average students are the least benefited ones among the three groups in terms of fostering Fluency - a component of creativity. Summary table of ANOVA according to gender with reference to fluency is given in table 4.3.

Table 4.3 Summary table of ANOVA of fluency by gender and treatments.

Source of Variation	df	SS	MS=SS/df	F	Significance
Gender (A)	2 - 1	9.5	9.5	0.19	No
Treatments (B)	2 - 1	4802	4802	97.48	Yes
Interaction (AB)	(2-1)(2-1)	-12.37	-12.37	-0.25	No
Within Groups (Error)	60 - (2)(2)	2758.66	49.26		

The obtained F-value with reference to factor AB (interaction) is -0.25 and the corresponding tabled value is 4.00 with df 1 and 56 at 0.05 level. Since the obtained F-value is less than the tabled value, it is not significant. This implies that there is no interaction between 'treatments' and 'gender'. Hence it may be concluded that Synectics model of teaching science is equally effective in fostering Fluency - a component of creativity for both male and female students.

Part - B

4.2.2 Analysis Pertaining to Flexibility - a Component of Creativity

In pursuance of objectives 2,7 and 12 i.e to find if there is significant difference between Synectics Model and Conventional Method of teaching science, in terms of fostering Flexibility - a component of Creativity and if there is any interaction between 'treatments' & 'levels' and 'treatments' & 'gender' with reference to fostering Flexibility - a component of Creativity, two-way analysis of variance was used. F-values obtained are presented in the summary Table 4.4 and Table 4.5.

(i) The obtained F-value with reference to factor B(treatments) is 33.72 and the corresponding tabled value is 7.17 with df 1 and 54 at 0.01 level. Since the obtained F-value is greater than the tabled value, it is significant. Therefore the corresponding null hypothesis stating that "there is no significant difference between Synectics model and Conventional method of teaching science with reference to fostering flexibility- a component of creativity" is rejected. Hence, it may be concluded that there is a significant difference between Synectics model and Conventional method of teaching science with reference to fostering of flexibility. Since the mean value of gain in flexibility scores of experimental group is greater than that of control group it may be interpreted that Synectics model of teaching science is more

Table 4.4 Summary table of ANOVA of Flexibility by Levels and Treatments

Source of Variation	df	SS	MS=SS/df	F	Significance
Levels (A)	3 - 1	22.9	11.45	0.28	No
Treatments (B)	2 - 1	1363.2	1363.2	33.72*	Yes
Interaction (AB)	(3-1)(2-1)	17.9	8.95	0.22	No
Within Groups (Error)	60 - (3)(2)	2183	40.43		

* Significant at 0.01 level.

Table 4.5 Summary table of ANOVA of Flexibility by Gender and Treatments

Source of Variation	df	SS	MS=SS/df	F	Significance
Gender (A)	2 - 1	38.25	38.25	2.21	No
Treatments (B)	2 - 1	985.63	985.63	56.81	Yes
Interaction (AB)	(2-1)(2-1)	34.13	34.13	1.97	No
Within Groups (Error)	60 - (2)(2)	971.62	17.35		

effective in fostering flexibility when compared to conventional method of teaching science.

(ii) The obtained F-value with reference to interaction is 0.22 which is less than the corresponding tabled value of 3.18

with df 2 and 54 at 0.05 level. Therefore, it may be concluded that the interaction between 'treatments' and 'levels' with reference to fostering flexibility is not significant.

In other words there is no interaction between 'treatments' and 'levels' i.e. Synectics model of teaching science is equally effective for all the three levels of students.

The obtained F-value with reference to factor AB(interaction) is 1.97 and the corresponding tabled value is 4.00 with df 1 and 56 at 0.05 level. Since the obtained F-value is less than the tabled value it is not significant. This implies that there is no interaction between 'treatments' and 'gender'.

Therefore it may be concluded that Synectics model of teaching science is equally effective in fostering flexibility - a component of creativity for both male and female students.

Part C

4.2.3 Analysis Pertaining to Originality - a Component of Creativity

In pursuance of objectives 3, 8 and 13 to find if there is significant difference between Synectics Model and Conventional Method of teaching science, in terms of fostering Originality - a component of Creativity and if there is any interaction between 'treatments' & 'levels' and 'treatments' & 'gender' with reference to fostering Originality - a component of Creativity, two-way analysis of variance was used for this purpose.

The gain scores of experimental and control groups according to levels with reference to Originality - a component of Creativity.

The corresponding F-values obtained are presented in the summary Table 4.6 and 4.7.

Table 4.6 Summary table of ANOVA of Originality by Levels and Treatments:

Source of Variation	df	SS	MS=SS/df	F	Significance
Levels (A)	3 - 1	194.2	97.1	1.36	No
Treatments (B)	2 - 1	4734.8	4734.8	66.49*	Yes
Interaction (AB)	(3-1)(2-1)	150.29	75.145	1.06	No
Within Groups (Error)	60 - (3)(2)	3845.3	71.21		

* Significant at 0.01 level.

Table 4.7 Summary table of ANOVA of Originality by Gender and Treatments.

Source of Variation	df	SS	MS=SS/df	F	Significance
Gender (A)	2 - 1	11.63	11.63	0.16	No
Treatments (B)	2 - 1	3874.25	3874.25	51.95	Yes
Interaction (AB)	(2-1)(2-1)	1.75	1.75	0.02	No
Within Groups (Error)	60 - (2)(2)	4176.23	74.58		

(i) The obtained F-value with reference to factor B(treatments) is 66.49 and the corresponding tabled value is 7.17 with df 1 and 54 at 0.01 level. Since the obtained F-value is greater than the tabled value, it is significant. Hence it may be concluded that there is a significant difference between Synectics model and Conventional method of teaching science with reference to fostering originality.

Since the mean value of gain in originality scores of experimental group is greater than that of the control group, it may be interpreted that Synectics model of teaching science is more effective in fostering originality when compared to Conventional method of teaching science.

(ii) The obtained F-value with reference to interaction is 1.06 which is less than the corresponding tabled value 3.18 with df 2 and 54 at 0.05 level. Therefore it may be concluded that the interaction between 'treatments' and 'levels' with reference to fostering originality is not significant.

In other words there is no interaction between 'treatments' and 'levels' i.e. Synectics model of teaching science is equally effective for all the three levels of students.

The obtained F-value with reference to factor AB(interaction) is 0.02 and the corresponding tabled value is 4.00 with df 1 and 56 at 0.05 level. Since the obtained F-value is less than the tabled value it is not significant. This implies that there is no interaction between 'treatments' and 'gender'

Hence it may be concluded that Synectics model of teaching science is equally effective in fostering originality - a component of Creativity for both male and female students.

Part D

4.2.4 Analysis Pertaining to Composite Creativity

In pursuance of objectives 4, 9 and 14 i.e, to find if there is significant difference between Synectics Model and Conventional Method of teaching science, in terms of fostering Composite Creativity and if there is any interaction between 'treatments' & 'levels' and 'treatments' & 'gender' with reference to fostering Composite Creativity, two-way analysis of variance was used.

The gain scores of experimental and control groups according to levels with reference to Composite Creativity .

The corresponidng F-values obtained are presented in the summary Table 4.8 and 4.9.

Table 4.8 Summary table of ANOVA of Composite Creativity by Levels and Treatments.

Source of Variation	df	SS	MS=SS/df	F	Significance
Levels (A)	3 - 1	925	462.5	2.27	No
Treatments (B)	2 - 1	34224.8	3422.8	167.73*	Yes
Interaction (AB)	(3-1)(2-1)	1044.5	522.25	2.56	No
Within Groups (Error)	60 - (3)(2)	11018.7	204.05		

* Significant at 0.01 level.

Table 4.9 Summary table of ANOVA of Composite Creativity by Gender and Treatments.

Source of Variation	df	SS	MS=SS/df	F	Significance
Gender (A)	2 - 1	236	236	0.19	No
Treatments (B)	2 - 1	26340.88	26340.88	21.47	Yes
Interaction (AB)	(2-1)(2-1)	15.88	15.88	0.01	No
Within Groups (Error)	60 - (2)(2)	68691.6	1226.64		

(i) The obtained F-value with reference to factor B(treatments) is 167.73 and the corresponding tabled value is 7.17 with df 1 and 54 at 0.01 level. Since the obtained F-value is greater than the tabled value, it is significant. Hence it may be concluded that there is a significant difference between Synectics model and Conventional method of teaching science with reference to fostering Creativity.

Since the mean value of gain in Creativity scores of experimental group is greater than that of the control group, it may be interpreted that Synectics model of teaching science is more effective in fostering Creativity when compared to Conventional method of teaching science.

(ii) The obtained F-value with reference to interaction is 2.56 which is less than the corresponding tabled value 3.18 with df 2 and 54 at 0.05 level. Therefore it may be concluded that the interaction between 'treatments' and 'levels' with reference to fostering creativity is not significant.

In other words there is no interaction between 'treatments' and 'levels' i.e. Synectics model of teaching science is equally effective for all the three levels of students.

The obtained F-value with reference to factor AB(interaction) is 0.01 and the corresponding tabled value is 4.00 with df 1 and 56 at 0.05 level. Since the obtained F-value is less than the tabled value it is not significant. This implies that there is no interaction between 'treatments' & 'gender'

Hence it may be concluded that Synectics model of teaching science is equally effective in fostering Creativity for both male and female students.

SECTION - 3

4.3 Analysis Pertaining to Problem Solving Ability

In pursuance of objectives 5, 10 and 15 i.e, to find if there is significant difference between Synectics Model and Conventional Method of teaching science, in terms of inducing problem solving ability and if there is any interaction between 'treatments' & 'levels' and 'treatments' & 'gender' with reference to inducing problem solving ability, two-way analysis of variance was used.

The gain scores of experimental and control groups according to levels with reference to Problem Solving Ability.

The corresponding F-values obtained are presented in the summary table 4.10 and 4.11.

Table 4.10 Summary table of ANOVA of Problem Solving Ability by Levels and Treatments.

Source of Variation	df	SS	MS=SS/df	F	Significance
Levels (A)	3 - 1	22.9	11.45	0.97	No
Treatments (B)	2 - 1	976.1	976.1	82.72*	Yes
Interaction (AB)	(3-1)(2-1)	39.4	19.7	1.67	No
Within Groups (Error)	60 - (3)(2)	637	11.8		

* Significant at 0.01 level.]

Table 4.11 Summary table of ANOVA of Problem Solving Ability by Gender and Treatments.

Source of Variation	df	SS	MS=SS/df	F	Significance
Gender (A)	2 - 1	13.38	13.38	1.09	No
Treatments (B)	2 - 1	799	799	64.96	Yes
Interaction (AB)	(2-1)(2-1)	26.88	26.88	2.18	No
Within Groups (Error)	60 - (2)(2)	689.04	12.3		

(i) The obtained F-value with reference to factor B(treatments) is 82.72 and the corresponding tabled value is 7.17 with df 1 and 54 at 0.01 level. Since the obtained F-value is greater than the tabled value, it is significant. Hence it may be concluded that there is a significant difference between Synectics model and Conventional method of teaching science with reference to inducing Problem Solving Ability

Since the mean value of gain in Problem Solving Ability scores of experimental group is greater than that of the control group, it may be interpreted that Synectics model of teaching science is more effective in inducing Problem Solving Ability when compared to Conventional method of teaching science.

(ii) The obtained F-value with reference to interaction is 1.67 which is less than the corresponding tabled value 3.18 with df 2 and 54 at 0.05 level. Therefore it may be concluded that the interaction between 'treatments' and 'levels' with reference to inducing Problem Solving Ability is not significant.

In other words there is no interaction between 'treatments' and 'levels' i.e. Synectics model of teaching science is equally effective for all the three levels of students.

The obtained F-value with reference to factor AB(interaction) is 2.18 and the corresponding tabled value is 4.00 with df 1 and 56 at 0.05 level. Since the obtained F-value is less than the tabled value it is not significant. This implies that there is no interaction between 'treatments' & 'gender'

Hence it may be concluded that Synectics model of teaching science is equally effective in inducing Problem Solving Ability for both male and female students.

SECTION -4

4.4 Analysis of Data Pertaining to Sustainment of Effects of the Treatment

From the analysis in the previous sections, 4.1, 4.2 and 4.3 it is found that Synectic model of teaching science is more effective than the Conventional method with reference to all the dependent variables. Further, it essential to test whether the effects of this treatment are sustainable by the students of the experimental group.

In pursuance of the objectives 16 to 20 i.e, to investigate whether the experimental group students sustain Fluency, Flexibility, Originality- components of creativity, Composite

Creativity and problem solving ability fostered through Synectics model of teaching science, t-test was used. For this the immediate post-test scores and delayed post-test scores of the experimental group were compared variable-wise by applying t-test. The following formula was used for computing t.

$$t = \frac{\Sigma d}{\sqrt{\frac{n\Sigma d^2 - (\Sigma d)^2}{n-1}}} \quad \text{with } df(n-1)$$

The results of the above analysis related to sustainment of the effects of treatments are given below in the summary table 4.12.

Table 4.12 : Summary Table of obtained 't' value and their significance.

Sl. No.	Dependent Variable	df	Obtained 't'	Tabled 't'	Significance
1	Fluency -component of Creativity	29	1.55	2.04	NS*
2	Flexibility - component of Creativity	29	1.9	2.04	NS*
3	Originality - component of Creativity	29	-0.26	2.04	NS*
4	Composite Creativity	29	0.77	2.04	NS*
5	Problem Solving Ability	29	1.52	2.04	NS*

NS* - Not significant

Since the obtained 't' value 1.55 with reference to fluency is less than the table 't' value 2.04 with df 29 at 0.05 level of significance, the difference is not significant. Similarly from the above table it is evident that the obtained 't' values with reference of flexibility, originality, composite creativity and problem solving ability are less than the corresponding table values with df 29 at 0.05 level of significance. Hence they are not significant.

This implies the following:

1. Immediate post-test and delayed post-test scores of experimental group donot differ significantly with reference to Fluency - a component of Creativity. Therefore it may be concluded that Fluency - a component of Creativity which is fostered through Synectics model of teaching is sustainable by the students.

2. Immediate post-test and delayed post-test scores of experimental group donot differ significantly with reference to Flexibility - a component of Creativity. Therefore it may be concluded that Flexibility- a component of Creativity which is fostered through Synectics model of teaching is sustainable by the students.

3. Immediate post-test and delayed post-test scores of experimental group donot differ significantly with reference to Originality - a component of Creativity. Therefore it may be concluded that Originality - a component of Creativity which is fostered through Synectics model of teaching is sustainable by the students.

4. Immediate post-test and delayed post-test scores of experimental group donot differ significantly with reference to Creativity. Therefore it may be concluded that Creativity which is fostered though Synectics model of teaching is sustainable by the students.

5. Immediate post-test and delayed post-test scores of experimental group donot differ significantly with reference to Problem Solving Ability. Therefore it may be concluded that Problem Solving Ability which is fostered though Synectics model of teaching is sustainable by the students.

SECTION - 5

4.5 Researcher's File

Till now, the data collected was analysed and interpretations were drawn based on quantitative analysis. To give a view of what really happened in the class room and the reactions of the students towards a new approach like Synectics approach to teach science, the following changes noted by the researcher are presented here.

At first, the students just looked towards the researcher with eager faces during the first sessions of stretching exercises on analogies. After an example was given some students started participating but many were hesitant to participate. In the next session almost all the students have shown eagerness to participate and the researcher even had problems in controlling the over participation of students so that the neighbouring classes would not be disturbed. By the time the sessions of Synectic approach adopted to science topics were started, the students were freely participating and fluently came out with interesting analogies.

They were so much interested with this type of teaching approach that they started asking the researcher to continue with another topic and to even engage the next period also. This approach of teaching was talked about with other sections by the experimental group students. Though the treatment was for a duration of just two months, the students were so much impressed that the students sent the investigator a greeting card on Teacher's day and thanked the researcher for making learning so easy, enjoyable, interesting and playful. The class teacher of the experimental group later even called up to the researcher and told her that the researcher was called analogy teacher by the students and the students were suggesting analogies to other topics in regular classes. It could thus be concluded that Synectics approach could certainly be used to make teaching - learning more interesting and playful and thus develop Creativity and Problem Solving Ability.

5

Summary and Conclusions -A Quick Bite

5.1 Introduction

Today the world is facing three major problems-population, pollution and poverty . Although science and technology have improved the lot of large number of human beings some of the worst problems of humanity such as mentioned above have been brought about or aggravated by science and technology. Education is one of the potent instruments in the development process, if it is properly geared for that purpose. Science education being an important component of education system should contribute in the solution of the problems by developing desirable understandings, skills, abilities and attitudes. The greatest challenge is to humanize science.

Now science has been dominating almost every field of our activities. Every country is trying to go ahead of the others in providing new way of life, which serves as timely warning to our country to reorient science education, so that we can attain a status of equality in the comity of nations and face the world with confidence and dignity.

Science is a cumulative and endless series of empirical observations, which result in the formation of concepts and theories with both concepts and theories being subject to modifications in the light of further empirical observations.

Science is both a body of knowledge and the process of acquiring and refining knowledge. Science is both a product and a process.

Science education should be designed so as to develop in the child well-defined abilities and values such as problem solving, creativity, objectivity and aesthetic sensibility. Through the teaching of science we have to develop the ability to learn independently and to enjoy the learning of science. It is therefore, important that new techniques and models of teaching should be adopted by teachers in order to make teaching of science more effective and efficient.

A model of teaching is a plan or pattern that can be used to shape curriculum, to design instructional material and to guide instruction in the classroom and other settings. Joyce and Weil (1980) designed more than twenty five models of teaching and classified them into four families viz.,

— Information processing models

— Social interaction models

— Personal models

— Behavior modification models

The information processing models emphasize ways of enhancing the human beings innate drive to make sense of the world by acquiring and organizing data, sensing problems and generating solutions to them, and developing concepts and language to convey them. Some generate creative thinking. A few enhance general intellectual ability. These models are useful for studying the self and society, thus for achieving the personal and social goals of education. Synectics model belongs to this family.

William.J.J. Gordon and his associates designed Synectics, an interesting approach to the development of creativity. Analogies is the chief element of Synectics. In Synectics exercises students 'play' with analogies until they relax and begin to enjoy making more and more metaphoric comparisons. Then they use analogies to attack problems or ideas. It is designed to lead students into a slightly illogical world to give us the opportunity to invent new ways of seeing things, expressing ourselves and approaching problems. There are two strategies based on Synectics procedure. The first strategy is designed to make the familiar strange and the second strategy is designed to make new unfamiliar ideas more meaningful.

Synectics model of teaching is moderately structured with the trainer initiating the sequence and guiding the use of operational mechanism. Norms of co-operation ,"play of fancy", intellectual and emotional equality are essential to establishing the setting for creative problem solving. The model contains strong elements of both instructional and nurturant values.

5.2 Need and Importance of the Study

Science is the product of creative thinking by scientists over a period of time. Children tend to be naturally creative, but their creativity is dampened as a result of authoritarian system of education. In the conventional method of teaching science there is very little chance to discover and foster the creative potentials of children. The discovery and development of creative genius of our youth should be the prime importance of our education. Teachers and educators, therefore, have a great responsibility to children and society to see that this ability is manifested to the maximum of the individual's potential.

At present, teaching of science has become rather content oriented. Learning of science has been diluted to mere acquisition of knowledge and information about scientific facts, principles, laws and theories. But the prime objective of teaching science in individualistic perspective is to impart the ability to use the scientific method of problem solving and the technique of observation and experimentation in handling problems of life. Hence special efforts are needed to develop creativity and problem solving ability among secondary school children through specially designed models.

Synectics model of teaching aims at developing creativity in children. One of its important side effects as claimed is it also develops problem solving ability. There is a need to test its effectiveness in terms of developing creativity and problem solving ability in children. Hence the present study was undertaken.

In addition to the above, a review of related literature highlights the fact that Indian studies related to this model of teaching especially using the second strategy i.e. making strange familiar and that too for science are far and few which makes the study significant.

5.3 Statement of the Problem

The problem chosen for the study is as mentioned below:

" A Study of Effectiveness of Synectics Model of teaching science on Creativity and Problem Solving Ability of Secondary School Students".

5.4 Review of Related Literature

The studies reviewed have been classified broadly into seven groups. They are:

1. Studies related to models of teaching in general.
2. Studies related to training strategy for models of teaching.
3. Studies related to developing models for teaching.
4. Studies related to fostering creativity.
5. Studies related to inducing problem solving ability.

6. Studies related to role of analogies in learning.

7. Studies related to Synectics model of teaching.

5.4.1 Insights from the Review

Educational research in general and research in the field of models of teaching in particular, are of recent origin. It is hopeful sign that research on models of teaching is generally receiving due importance.

The overview of the researches related to 'models of teaching', 'fostering creativity' and 'inducing problem solving ability' crystallised some of the issues and observations that may help in framing hypotheses, selection of tools for collecting data, sampling techniques, adopting experimental design and employing statistical techniques for analysis of data for the present study. It was observed that studies on models of teaching were by and large based on experimental designs. Most of the experiments have been carried out in actual classroom settings and are quasi experimental. Designing such studies in the classroom situation has an advantage of assessing the effectiveness of a teaching strategy in real conditions. It was also observed that creative thinking and ability to solve problems could be enhanced by disciplined procedures like training in creative problem solving, creative writing exercises etc.

From the review it was found that there were very few studies conducted on Synectics Model of teaching. Those which were available adopted the model for teaching in the subject of languages like Hindi and English. Though an action research was taken up by Anandi Martis and D'hima(1987) on Synectics model of teaching science, its effect on composite creativity was found. The components of creativity like fluency, flexibility and originality were not studied separately.

There are two strategies of teaching in Synectics model. The first strategy refers to 'making familiar strange'(MFS) and the second strategy refers to 'making strange familiar'(MSF). Most of the studies have adopted the first strategy. The second strategy i.e. the MSF approach has rarely been adopted. One study by Anandi Martis was taken up to develop MSF competencies through Synectics model of teaching in graduate student teachers. It was observed that there is no study on Synectics model of teaching science adopting the MSF approach at secondary school level in Indian settings. It was also observed that development of problem solving ability which is an important side effect of Synectics model of teaching is not at all studied. Hence the present investigation is a modest venture in this direction.

5.5 General Objectives of the Study

The following are the broad objectives of the study

1. Compare the effectiveness of Synectics Model and Conventional Method of teaching science in terms of fostering Fluency, Flexibility and Originality-components of Creativity and Composite Creativity
2. Compare the effectiveness of Synectics Model and Conventional Method of teaching science in terms of inducing Problem Solving Ability.
3. Investigate interaction between 'treatments' and 'levels of students' with reference to fostering Fluency, Flexibility, Originality-components of Creativity and Composite Creativity
4. Investigate interaction between 'treatments' and 'levels of students' with reference to inducing Problem Solving Ability.
5. Investigate interaction between 'treatments' and 'gender' with reference to fostering Fluency, Flexibility, Originality - components of Creativity and composite Creativity,

6. Investigate interaction between 'treatments' and 'gender' with reference to inducing Problem Solving Ability.

7. Investigate whether the students sustain Fluency, Flexibility, Originality-components of Creativity and Composite Creativity fostered through Synectics Model of teaching science.

8. Investigate whether the students sustain Problem Solving Ability induced through Synectics Model of teaching science.

5.6 Hypotheses of the Study

The following major hypotheses were formulated in pursuance of the broad objectives of the study:

1. Synectics Model is more effective than the Conventional Method of teaching science in terms of fostering Fluency, Flexibility, Originality and Composite Creativity.

2. Synectics Model is more effective than the Conventional Method of teaching science in terms of inducing Problem Solving Ability.

3. There is interaction between 'treatments' and 'levels' with reference to fostering Fluency, Flexibility, Originality and Composite Creativity.

4. There is interaction between 'treatments' and 'levels' with reference to inducing Problem Solving Ability.

5. There is interaction between 'treatments' and 'gender' with reference to fostering Fluency, Flexibility, Originality and Composite Creativity.

6. There is interaction between 'treatments' and 'gender' with reference to inducing Problem Solving Ability.

7. Immediate and delayed post test scores of the experimental group differ significantly with reference to Fluency, Flexibility, Originality and Composite Creativity.

8. Immediate and delayed post test scores of the experimental group differ significantly with reference to Problem Solving Ability.

5.7 Variables of the Study

The variables used in the study are classified into independent, dependent and moderate variables.

(i) Independent Variable

- Treatments viz., (a) Synectics Model of Teaching Science
  (b) Conventional Method of Teaching Science.

(ii) Dependent variables

- Fluency
- Flexibility
- Originality
- Composite Creativity
- Problem Solving Ability.

(iii) Moderate variables

- Levels of students
- Gender

5.8 Design of the Experiment

The study was experimental in nature. The investigator followed pre-test post-test parallel group experimental design

The procedure followed to conduct the experiment is diagrammatically shown below.

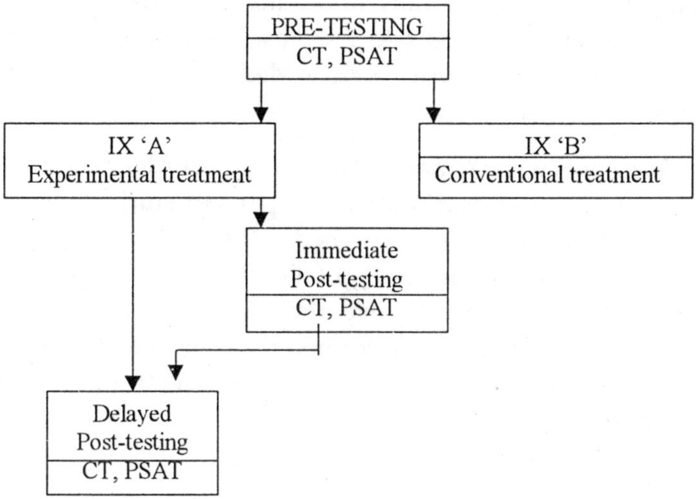

5.9 Sampling Procedure

Multistage purposive sampling technique was employed for the study. A suitable school where the experiment could be conducted was identified. The researcher selected Florence High School located in Bangalore City by keeping the following points in view:

- The willing co-operation of the head of the institution and members of the staff.
- The strength of students in the class.
- Regularity of pupils attending the class.

IX standard was considered to be the suitable class both from academic and administrative point of view for conducting the experiment.

For obtaining two parallel groups the students were matched on intellectual capacity and higher mental ability in science. Hence 50 students of each division of IX standard were administered Standard Progressive Matrices(SPM) and Test of Higher Mental Ability in Science(THMAS). Both the test scores were converted into T scores. Then the obtained T scores on SPM and THMAS were added to get a composite T score.

The scores were arranged in descending order classwise and exactly or most nearly matching pairs of students were identified. From this thirty matched pairs of students were obtained. This formed the sample of the study. Thirty students of one division formed the experimental group and thirty students of the other division formed the control group. This was done by random selection. This is diagrammatically shown below.

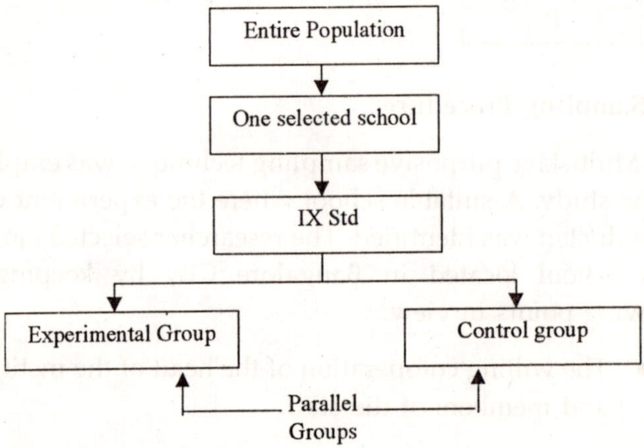

5.10 Tools used for the Study

The following tools were used for the study

I) Tools adopted

The following tools were adopted in view of the need of the present study.

(i) Standard Progressive Matrices(SPM)

............Raven(1938)

Reliability

Test-Retest : 0.8 to 0.93

Consistency Reliability : 0.87 to 0.97

Validity : has concurrent validity

(ii) Test for Higher Mental Ability in Science(THMAS)

............Sansanwal & Anuradha Joshi (1989)

Reliability

Test-Retest Reliability : 0.8 to 0.93

Validity : has concurrent validity

iii) Verbal test of Creative thinking(VTCT)

............Baqer Mehdi (1973)

Reliability

Test-Retest Reliability: 0.896 to 0.59

Validity : has concurrent validity

II) Tool developed

The following tool was developed by the investigator for the study

Problem Solving Ability Test(PSAT)

Reliability

Test-Retest Reliability : 0.75

Split half : 0.92

Validity : The test has concurrent validity

5.11 Statistical Techniques Employed

The following statistical techniques were used to analyse the collected data :

(i) Two-way Analysis of variance : The principle involved in the analysis of variance is the comparison of variability between the various groups within the sum of variability found within the groups. As two-way analysis of variance permits the simultaneous study of two factors as well as interaction between the two, this technique was used for the purpose of analysis of data.

(ii) t-test: t-test was used to know whether the experimental and control groups differ on the dependent variables initially i.e. before applying the treatments. It was also used to know whether the immediate post-test and delayed post-test scores differ significantly with reference to dependent variables.

5.12 Major Findings of the Study-For those Who Value Discoveries

The major findings of the study are :

1. Synectics model of teaching science is more effective than the conventional method in fostering Fluency - a component of Creativity.

2. Synectics model of teaching science is more effective than the conventional method in fostering Flexibility - a component of Creativity.

3. Synectics model of teaching science is more effective than the conventional method in fostering Originality - a component of Creativity.

4. Synectics model of teaching science is more effective than the conventional method of fostering Composite Creativity.

5. Synectics model of teaching science is more effective than the conventional method in inducing Problem Solving Ability.

6. Synectics model of teaching science differs in its effectiveness for the three levels of students in fostering Fluency - a component of Creativity. The above average students are more benefited when compared to average and below average students. Average students are moderately benefited and the below average students are the least benefited ones among the three groups.

7. Synectics model of teaching science is equally effective for all the three levels of students in fostering Flexibility - a component of Creativity.

8. Synectics model of teaching science is equally effective for all the three levels of students in fostering Originality- a component of Creativity.

9. Synectics model of teaching science is equally effective for all the three levels of students in fostering Composite Creativity.

10. Synectics model of teaching science is equally effective for all the three levels of students in inducing Problem Solving Ability.

11. Synectics model of teaching science is equally effective for both boys and girls in fostering Fluency- a component of Creativity.

12. Synectics model of teaching science is equally effective for both boys and girls in fostering Flexibility- a component of Creativity.

13. Synectics model of teaching science is equally effective for both boys and girls in fostering Originality - a component of Creativity.

14. Synectics model of teaching science is equally effective for both boys and girls in fostering Composite Creativity.

15. Synectics model of teaching science is equally effective for both boys and girls in developing Problem Solving Ability.

16. The students sustain Fluency - a component of Creativity fostered through Synectics model of teaching science.

17. The students sustain Flexibility- a component of Creativity fostered through Synectics model of teaching science.

18. The students sustain Originality - a component of Creativity fostered through Synectics model of teaching science.

19. The students sustain Composite Creativity fostered through Synectics model of teaching science.

20. The students sustain Problem Solving Ability induced through Synectics model of teaching science.

5.13 Educational Implications of the Study-Need of the Day

The following are the educational implications of the present study :

1. It is found that Synectics model of teaching is more effective than the conventional method of teaching in developing fluency, flexibility and originality components of creativity and composite creativity as a whole. Therefore Synectics sessions may be successfully organised in schools to facilitate the development of creativity.

2. It is found that Synectics model is effective in developing problem solving ability among the students. This model may be used successfully to develop problem solving ability which is very essential for students.

3. It was found that Synectics model differed in its effectiveness in fostering fluency for above average, average and below average students. Hence the students may be segregated in the classroom on the basis of their levels for developing fluency.

4. Synectics model was equally effective for all the three levels of students in developing flexibility, originality, composite creativity and problem solving ability. They need not be segregated based on their levels in the classroom for this purpose.

5. Synectics model of teaching science was equally effective for both boys and girls in fostering fluency, flexibility and originality components of creativity, composite creativity and problem solving ability. Hence boys and girls need not be segregated in the classroom on the basis of their gender.

6. By the investigator's experience with Synectics model of teaching it was seen that it could be easily be adopted to secondary school students in the existing Indian classroom.

7. One of the goals of effective teaching i.e. equality of learning opportunity could be provided by adopting this model.

8. While adopting Synectics model for teaching a set of well organized questions needs to be asked so as to lead the students to think in the right direction.

9. The current science text books of secondary schools may be analyzed and topics which could be taught by Synectics model could be pointed out. The analogies which could be used for these topics could also be suggested in the text books.

10. The students enjoy playing with analogies in a

Synectics lesson. They actively participate in the classroom discourses. They also suggest their own analogies to a topic and play with these analogies. Occasionally this game can be practiced in the classrooms which ensures the development of creativity and problem solving ability.

11. As the model requires the student to participate actively in suggesting and comparing analogies, it helps in improving their language ability.

12. Training programmes on Synectics model could be organised for pre-service and in-service teachers so as to develop an understanding and the necessary skills for the successful implementation of the model in the classroom situation.

13. The teacher educators must also be trained in Synectics model of teaching, so that they are competent enough to train students teachers in Synectics model.

14. Models of teaching are to be included in the curriculum at TCH, B.Ed and M.Ed levels. The student teachers are to be taught with the theory of the models of teaching and should also be allowed to practice the models of teaching.

5.14 Suggestions for Further Research-Where the Study Never Ends

Based on the present study, the researcher felt the need for undertaking the following studies in this field:

1. A study to find the effectiveness of Synectics model in terms of both instructional and nurturant effects could be undertaken.

2. Similar study could be conducted with larger samples. Similar studies could be conducted on students of different classes viz., VII and X.

3. A long term experimental study (of atleast one academic session duration), may be planned on the same lines and design, to study the effects of Synectics model of teaching.

4. The present study was undertaken in English on English medium students. The Synectics model of teaching can also be tried on Kannada medium students.

5. The sample considered for the present studying is urban sample. The experiment can be tried on rural sample too.

6. Studies may be conducted to investigate the duration of treatment needed for the development of creativity and problem solving ability in above average, average and below average students.

7. Studies could be undertaken to develop valid and reliable tools for assessing the instructional and nuturant effects of Synectics model of teaching.

8. Similar studies could be undertaken to investigate the effectiveness of Synectics model in different school subjects like Mathematics, Language, History and Geography.

9. The effectiveness of Synectics model of teaching under the individual and the collaborative learning modes on creativity and problem solving ability could be studied.

10. A study to investigate the interaction effects of Synectics model with other personal family models such as non-directive teaching, Awareness training and Classroom meeting could be undertaken.

11. Studies to investigate the interaction effects of Synectics

model with other variables such as personality factors, SES, achievement motivation etc, and development of creativity and problem solving ability could be undertaken.

12. Studies to develop training strategies for teachers in Synectics model, to develop competencies in handling the model could be taken up .

6

Educational Implications and Suggestions For Further Research

Educational Implications of the Study—Need of the Day

The following are the educational implications of the present study:

1. It is found that Synectics model of teaching is more effective than the conventional method of teaching in developing fluency, flexibility and originality components of creativity and composite creativity as a whole. Therefore Synectics sessions may be successfully organised in schools to facilitate the development of creativity.

2. It is found that Synectics model is effective in developing problem solving ability among the students. This model may be used successfully to develop problem solving ability which is very essential for students.

3. It was found that Synectics model differed in its effectiveness in fostering fluency for above average, average and below average students. Hence the students may be segregated in the classroom on the basis of their levels for developing fluency.

4. Synectics model was equally effective for all the three levels of students in developing flexibility,

originality, composite creativity and problem solving ability. They need not be segregated based on their levels in the classroom for this purpose.

5. Synectics model of teaching science was equally effective for both boys and girls in fostering fluency, flexibility and originality components of creativity, composite creativity and problem solving ability. Hence boys and girls need not be segregated in the classroom on the basis of their gender.

6. By the investigator's experience with Synetics model of teaching it was seen that it could be easily be adopted to secondary school students in the existing Indian classroom.

7. One of the goals of effective teaching i.e. equality of learning opportunity could be provided by adopting this model.

8. While adopting Synectics model for teaching a set of well organized questions needs to be asked so as to lead the students to think in the right direction.

9. The current science text books of secondary schools may be analyzed and topics which could be taught by Synectics model could be pointed out. The analogies which could be used for these topics could also be suggested in the text books.

10. The students enjoy playing with analogies in a Synectics lesson. They actively participate in the classroom discourses. They also suggest their own analogies to a topic and play with these analogies. Occasionally this game can be practiced in the classrooms wihich ensures the development of creativity and problem solving ability.

11. As the model requires the student to participate

actively in suggesting and comparing analogies, it helps in improving their language ability.

12. Training programmes on Synectics model could be organised for pre-service and in-service teachers so as to develop an understanding and the necessary skills for the successful implementation of the model in the classroom situation.

13. The teacher educators must also be trained in Synectics model of teaching, so that they are competent enough to train students teachers in Synetics model.

14. Models of teaching are to be included in the curriculum at TCH, B.Ed and M.Ed levels. The student teachers are to be taught with the theory of the models of teaching should also be allowed to practice the models of teaching.

Suggestions for Further Research-Where the Study Never Ends

Based on the present study, the researcher felt the need for undertaking the following studies in this field:

1. A study to find the effectiveness of Synectics model in terms of both instructional and nurturant effects could be undertaken.

2. Similar study could be conducted with larger samples. Similar studies could be conducted on students of different classes viz., VII and X.

3. A long term experimental study (of atleast one academic session duration), may be planned on the same lines and design, to study the effects of Synectics model of teaching.

4. The present study was undertaken in English on

English medium students. The Synectics model of teaching can also be tried on Kannada medium students.

5. The sample considered for the present study is urban sample. The experiment can be tried on rural sample too.

6. Studies may be conducted to investigate the duration of treatment needed for the development of creativity and problem solving ability in above average, average and below average students.

7. Studies could be undertaken to develop valid and reliable tools for assessing the instructional and nuturant effects of Synectics model of teaching.

8. Similar studies could be undertaken to investigate the effectiveness of Synetics model in different school subjects like Mathematics, Language, History and Geography.

9. The effectiveness of Synectics model of teaching under the individual and the collaborative learning modes on creativity and problem solving ability could be studied.

10. A study to investigate the interaction effects of Synectics model with other personal family models such as non-directive teaching, Awareness training and Classroom meeting could be undertaken.

11. Studies to investigate the interaction effects of Synectics model with other variables such as personality factors, SES, achievement motivation etc., and development of creativity and problem solving ability could be undertaken.

12. Studies to develop training strategies for teachers in Synectics model, to develop competencies in handling the model could be taken up.

APPENDICES

APPENDIX - A

PROBLEM SOLVING ABILITY TEST(PSAT)

Name : ______________ School: ________________

Sex : ____________________ Class : ________________

Instructions:

This booklet consists of some problem episodes which you might have also experienced in your day to day life. Read them carefully and write your responses regarding each heading given below each episode. You are free to suggest as many solutions as you can for each problem You may seek clarification if you have any doubts with any of the problem episodes.

Here is an example below to help you that what you are expected to do with this booklet.

Problem episodes

You want to cross a river from south to north. You cannot swim, no boats are available and the only way you could reach the other side is by walking across the bridge there, but it is flooded by water. You are not able to see the bridge at all. How would you cross the river using the bridge ?

a) Define the problem :

How would I cross the river when the bridge is flooded?

b) Clues identified to arrive at the solution :

— I have to cross the river

— I cannot swim

— No boats are available

— There is a bridge which is flooded and by which I can cross the river

— I am not able to see the bridge

c) ***Solution arrived*** :

With the help of a stick I will find the way on the bridge and walk across it.

1) A flask which has boiling water is kept on a table. A balloon is given to you, without actually blowing air into the balloon it has to be expanded. How will you do it ?

a) Define the problem :

____

____

____

b) Clues identified to arrive at the solution :

____

____

____

c) Solution :

____

____

____

2) You are given two blades and asked to put these into water such that one blade floats and the other drowns. How would you do it ?

a) Define the problem:

____

____

____

b) Clues identified to arrive at the solution :

____

____

____

c) Solution :

____

____

____

3) A mug is tied to the free end of a piece of string that has been attached to some support above. You have to cut the string anywhere above the mug without the mug falling. How would you do it ?

a) Define the problem:

____

____

____

b) Clues identified to arrive at the solution :

____

c) Solution :

4) A lighted candle is kept on a table, you have to put off the candle light without blowing the flame or touching it. How will you do it ?

a) Define the problem:

b) Clues identified to arrive at the solution :

c) Solution :

5) You have gone to a market place. The path is very narrow. There you come across three cycles passing the path from the opposite direction. To avert a clash what solution would you suggest.

a) Define the problem:

____

____

____

b) Clues identified to arrive at the solution :

____

____

____

c) Solution :

____

____

____

6) You have gone to the canteen with your friends. One of your friends keeps a coin on the floor and inverts a cup over it. He asks you to remove the coin without touching the cup. How would you do that ?

a) Define the problem:

____

____

____

b) Clues identified to arrive at the solution :

____

____

____

c) Solution :

____

____

____

7) When Nisha was working in the lab she spilt iron fillings into a plate filled with saw dust. She asks for your help to separate the iron fillings from the saw dust. How would you do it easily ?

a) Define the problem:

____

____

____

b) Clues identified to arrive at the solution :

____

____

____

c) Solution :

____

____

____

8) You have gone to a picnic with your friends. You and two of your friends are sleeping under a tree. A prankster has smeared charcoal on all three of your faces. When you woke up all three of you burst out laughing . At first none of you release that your own face is dirty. Later you stop laughing. How did you come to know that your face is also smeared ?

a) Define the problem:

____

____

____

b) Clues identified to arrive at the solution :

____

____

____

c) Solution :

____

____

____

9) You are playing with your friends. One of your friends held up two fullscape sheets on the same size, one in each hand. He asks you to drop them simultaneously from the same height, but on a condition that the paper in your right hand should reach the ground faster. How would you do this ?

a) Define the problem:

____

____

____

b) Clues identified to arrive at the solution :

____

____

____

c) Solution :

____

____

____

10) You are locked in a room on the second floor. You have to come out of the room. There is an open window through which you can come out. But the window is very far from the ground. To your luck you find a very thick, twined rope. You tie one end to the bars of the window and let the rope dangle down the wall. It reached half way. The gap is still too much. You cannot get anything to tie to it. But by using only the rope you have to get down. How will you do it?

a) Define the problem:

____

____

____

b) Clues identified to arrive at the solution :

____

____

____

c) Solution :

____

____

____

11) A deaf and dumb man came to you and asked for a

book. He could not speak. So he mimed to ask for the book. Then another deaf and dumb man came to you and mimed the gesture of writing, to ask for a pen. Then a blind man came. He wanted to ask for a box. What sort of gestures do you suppose he made to ask for a box?

a) Define the problem:

____

____

____

b) Clues identified to arrive at the solution :

____

____

____

c) Solution :

____

____

____

12) You are taking bath. Suddenly the tap breaks and the water starts gushing out. You try to leave the bathroom but you find the door is jammed. The drainage pipe from which the water is going out is also blocked. There is a window which is closed and you cannot reach it. The water starts raising in the room. Soon it reaches your chin. You become desperate. What would you do to save your life ?

a) Define the problem:

____

b) Clues identified to arrive at the solution :

c) Solution :

13) You are playing in a garden where a gardener is watering the plants with a pipe. Your tennis ball falls into a deep hole. Your hand cannot reach down and a bend in the middle of the hole makes it impossible for you to retrieve the ball with the help of sticks. How would you get the ball out ?

a) Define the problem:

b) Clues identified to arrive at the solution :

c) Solution :

14) A soldier has to cross a river. There is no bridge. The soldier sees two boys playing in a tiny row boat and he calls them. The boat can hold only 100kgs. The soldier weights 100kgs and the boys weigh 50 kgs each. Yet, using the boat all the three cross over. How?

a) Define the problem:

b) Clues identified to arrive at the solution :

c) Solution :

15) You are travelling in a train which is moving in northward direction. The seats are so arranged that you can sit facing the northward or the south ward direction. Many of the seats are unoccupied. You can choose to sit wherever you want. You are sitting facing the north . The wind is blowing very fast. You try to close the windows, but cannot. What would you do to avoid the wind ?

a) Define the problem:

____

____

____

b) Clues identified to arrive at the solution :

____

____

____

c) Solution :

____

____

____

APPENDIX - A(I)

DRAFT OF EPISODES OF PROBLEM SOLVING ABILITY TEST

INSTRUCTIONS :

We experience many problem - situations in our day-to-day life. This booklet consists of some problem - episodes which you might have experienced or you have witnessed that your friends might have experienced. Read them carefully one after the other and think to overcome these problems. You have to suggest solutions/ways and means to overcome the same. You are free to suggest as many solutions /way-outs as you could for each problem. You may also ask for clarification if you have any doubts.

EPISODES :

1. When you are playing in a garden, your tennis ball has

fallen into a deep hole. Your hand can't reach down and a bend in the middle of the hole makes it impossible for you to retrieve the ball with the help of sticks. No one is there to help you except the gardener who is watering the plants with a pipe. How would you get the ball out ?

2. You have gone to a party. Your friend keeps a coin on the floor and inverts a cup over it. He asks you to remove the coin without touching the cup. How can you do that?

3. You are playing with your friends. One of your friends held up two fullscape sheets of the same size, one in each hand. He asks you to drop them simultaneously from the same height, but on a condition that the paper in your right hand should reach the ground faster. How could you do this?

4. A basket of cherries is placed before you and your friend. A cloth is tied to your eyes and you cannot see, whereas your friend can see. Both of you are asked to eat only one cheery at a time. After some time you have a doubt that your friend is cheating you by taking two at a twice. Without removing the cloth tied, how would you find out whether your friend is cheating or not?

5. You have gone to a picnic with your friends. You and two of your friends are sleeping under a tree. A prankster has smeared charcoal on all three of your faces. When you woke-up all three of you burst out laughing. At first none of your release that your own face is dirty. Later one of your friend stops laughing. How did he come to know that his face is also smeared?

6. You are taking bath. Suddenly the tap breaks and the

water starts gushing out. You try to leave the bathroom but you find that the door is jammed. The pipe from which the water is going out is blocked. There is a window which is closed and you cannot reach it. The water starts raising in the room. Soon it reaches your chin. You become desperate. What would you do to save yourself?

7. You have a boat that will carry only 100kg. Your father, your brother and you have to cross the river. You father weights 100kgs. You and your brother each weigh 50kgs. How would you cross the river ?

8. Your sister tells you that she has learnt some magic. She asks you to look into a glass that she has placed in her palm. You can see a coin at the bottom of the glass. She covers the glass with a handkerchief and hands it over to you and asks you to uncover it. When the glass is uncovered you see that it is empty. She tells you that, she has made the coin disappear. She asks you also to do the same. How would you do it ?

9. You want to cross a river from South to North. You cannot swim, no boats are available and the only way you could reach the otherside is by walking across the bridge there. The bridge is guarded by a soldier who would not let anyone to use it. You, at first, thought it would be impossible to cross the bridge as the solider comes out of his hut every 5 minutes and it takes you at least 10 minutes to cross the bridge. How would you succeed this problem?

10. You are locked in a room on the second floor. You have to come out of the room. There is an open window through which you can come out. But the window is very far from the ground. To your luck you find a very thick (twined) rope. You tie one end to the bars of the window and let the rope dangle down the wall. It

reached half way. The gap is still too much. You cannot get anything to tie to it. But by using only the rope you have to get down. How will you do it?

11. Three girls are standing on the bank of a river. They are Asha, Kala and Chitra. A shot is fired on the other side. All the three notice it and argue that they were aware of the shot (first) before the other two. Asha says she saw the smoke from the gun, Chitra the puller strike the water and Kala heard the sound of the bullet. You are asked to decide who knew of it first. How will you decide about who knew of it first ?

12. You are travelling in a train which is moving in northward direction. The seats are so arranged that you can sit facing the northward or the southward direction. Many of the seats are unoccupied. You can choose to sit wherever you want. You are sitting facing the north. The wind is blowing very fast. You try to close the window, but cannot. What would you do to avoid the wind?

13. Two white workmen fell through a chimney and were unhurt. Without speaking a word or discussing their sudden fall both men started back to job. It happened that one man's face was well smeared with soot of chimney and the other man's face was very clean. Yet the man with the clean face went and washed his face, the man with dirty face went back tow work without washing his face? Can you explain logically why he did so?

14. A platoon of soldiers has to cross a river. There is no bridge. The platoon's officer sees two boys playing in a tiny row boat and he calls them. The boat can hold only the two boys or only one solider. It cannot hold a boy and soldier. Yet, using the boat the platoon crosses over .How ?

15. There is a rope which is hung over a weightless, frictionless pulley attached to the roof of a building. At one end of the rope is gold of 15 pound weight which exactly counter balances you at the other end. Below there is a river flowing. You should escape from the place with the gold. You do not know swimming. How would you get the gold and escape ?

16. You are given an uninflated balloon. Your friend draws a square on it. You have to give him the balloon with a bigger square on it. You are not allowed to draw anything on it. How would you do it?

17. Your mother has bought nine pearls all alike in size and appearance. The next day the jeweller from whom you have brought the pearls tells you that one of the pearls is a fake. He also tells you that the fake one weights less than the others. But he agrees to replace it with an original pearl if and only if you can find out the fake pearl in only two weighings. How will you do it?

18. When you are playing a game, your rival group doesnot want you to play as you are a very good player. So they thought of a plan. They put two pieces of paper in a covered basket. Then called 3 judges and told them they had written 'Go' on one of the piece and 'STAY' on the other. If you drew the piece marked 'STAY' you could play. You somehow come to know that the rival group has written 'GO' on both pieces of paper but without exposing that to the judges you have to get the decision in your favour. How could you do it?

19. A mug is tied to the free end of a piece of string that has been attached to some support above. You have to cut the string anywhere above the mug without the mug falling. How would you do it?

20. A deaf & dumb man came to you and asked for a book. He could not speak. So he mimed to ask for the book. Then another deaf and dumbman came and mimed the gesture of writing, to ask for a pen. Then a blindman came. He wanted to ask for a box. What sort of gestures do you suppose he made to ask for a box?

21. You are kidnapped and locked in a room. You want to escape from there. The door is heavily barred and well guarded and you cannot get out that way. You have a small dagger and can dig into the floor with it. But is useless to try to tunnel out because the walls which are made of concrete extend much below into the earth. The only opening is a small skylight in the middle of the ceiling 8 feet above. The room is absolute bare and there is nothing on which you can stand to reach the ceiling. How do you manage to get away?

22. In a workshop, a cutting player, a scissors, screw driver etc., have been kept on a table. Two ropes have been hung at two opposite corners of the room. The bottom ends of these ropes have to be tied. When you bring one end of a rope, the other one cannot be caught as the length of the rope is less. How would you connect these two ropes and tie them?

23. Your uncle put some ice-cubes in a net bag along with a stone and dropped the bag into a tall glass of water. Because of the stone, the bag sank to the bottom. He gives this to you and asks you to boil the water by heating such that the ice cubes remain unaffected. How would you do that ?

24. A man had one tiger, one goat and a bundle of grass and a boat. He had to cross from one bank of the river to the opposite bank with all these with the condition that he could take any one at a time with him. If he took the bundle of grass the tiger would eat the goat.

If he left the goat and grass he goat would eat the grass. Even on the other bank he could not leave the tiger and goat or the goat and the bundle of grass. How would he bring all the three to the other bank.

25. You have gone to a market place. The path is very narrow. There you come across three cycles passing the path from the opposite direction. To avert a clash what solution would you suggest ?

26. A flask which has boiling water is kept on a table. A balloon is given to you, without actually blowing air into the balloon it has to expanded. How will you do it ?

27. A lighted candle is kept on a table. You have to put off the candle light without blowing the flame or touching it. How will you do it.

28. You are given two blades and asked to put them into water such that one blade floats and the other drowns. How would you do it ?

29. A boat is filled to the brim such that even if a needle is placed in it, it would drown. But you have to still keep a big balloon in it. What will you do to keep the balloon without drowning the boat?

30. When Nisha was working in the Lab she spilt iron fillings into a plate filled with sawdust. She asks for your help to separate the iron fillings from the saw dust. How would you do it easily?

31. Anand and his family have gone to a desert. Anand has the habit of keeping a convex lens with him always. They are travelling on a camel. The day is very hot. They feel like drinking water. They see an Oasis. But Anand's father objects to drink that water, for the reason that it might not be good. So, they want to boil

the water before drinking. But they donot have a matchstick to light a fire. Later Anand collects some dry twigs and paper and lights the fire. How did he do it?

32. You forgot to bring your Bus-pass. You do not have money to take a ticket and travel in the bus, to reach your school in time. You can't go back home and bring money because your father and mother have left to their offices. But you have determined to reach your school in time which is at a distance of 3.5Kms. Only half an hour time is left out. How would you make it possible?

33. One of your friends shouts that some one has stolen his pen, for which no one in the class accepts his complaint. At last all of you agreed to check your bags and unfortunately it was found in your bag. You are an honest person and really you don't know how it has come into your bag. Your friend tells that, he will complain the matter to your class teacher. How would you try to prove yourself honest and the complaint baseless?

APPENDIX -A(II)
Calculation of Difficulty Index and Discriminatory Power of Items of PSAT

Item	Ph	Pl	Ph % R	Pl % R	P	D
1	12	6	92.31	46.15	0.69	0.46
2	9	5	69.23	38.46	0.54	0.31
3	11	5	84.6	38.46	0.62	0.46
4	7	2	53.9	15.39	0.35	0.46
5	10	5	76.9	38.46	0.58	0.39
6	12	5	92.31	38.46	0.65	0.54
7	12	5	92.31	38.46	0.65	0.54
8	6	1	46.15	7.69	0.27	0.39
9	7	0	53.85	0	0.27	0.54
10	12	4	92.31	30.77	0.62	0.62
11	10	9	76.9	69.23	0.73	0.08
12	13	8	100	61.54	0.81	0.39
13	8	2	61.54	15.39	0.39	0.46
14	12	6	92.31	46.15	0.69	0.46
15	4	2	30.77	15.39	0.23	0.15
16	2	0	15.39	0	0.07	0.15
17	8	0	61.54	0	0.31	0.61
18	10	1	76.92	7.69	0.42	0.69
19	12	5	92.31	38.46	0.65	0.53
20	5	2	38.46	15.39	0.27	0.23
21	0	0	0	0	0	0
22	0	0	0	0	0	0
23	1	0	7.69	0	0.04	0.08
24	11	3	84.62	23.08	0.54	0.62
25	9	0	69.23	0	0.35	0.69
26	13	1	100	7.69	0.53	0.92
27	10	0	76.92	0	0.39	0.77
28	0	0	0	0	0	0
29	12	2	92.31	15.39	0.54	0.77
30	2	0	15.39	0	0.77	0.15
31	2	1	15.39	7.69	0.12	0.08

Index of Discrimination	Item Evaluation
0.40 & up	Very good items
0.30 to 0.39	Reasonably good but possible subject to improvement
0.20 to 0.29	Marginal items, usually needing and being subject to improvement.
Below 0.19	Poor items, to be rejected or improved by revision

Item difficulty 0.5 to 0.7 i.e. 50% to 70% is acceptable.

APPENDIX A(III - a)

Test-Retest Reliability of PSAT

Test Scores 'X' variable (PSAT)

C.I.	0-9	10-19	20-29	30-39	40-49	50-59	60-69		y^1	fy^1	$(fy^1)^2$	Σfx^1y^1 — +
60-69						1111 ~~0~~ / 0	~~1~~ 1 / 1	6	1	6		1
50-59				111 0 / 0	1111 ~~0~~ / 0	11111 ~~0~~ / 0	~~1~~ 0 / 0	15	0	0		0
40-49			11 3 / 6	1111 2 / 8	1 1 / 1	11 0 / 0		9	-1	-9		15
30-39	1 10 / 10	11 8 / 16	1111 ~~6~~ / 30	111 4 / 12	1 2 / 2			12	-2	-24		70
20-29		1 12 / 12	11 9 / 18		1 3 / 3			4	-3	-12		33
10-19												
0-9												
fx	1	3	9	10	8	13	2	46		Σfy^1 -39	$\Sigma(fy^1)^2$ 99	Σfx^1y^1 119
x^1	-5	-4	-3	-2	-1	0	1					
fx^1	-5	-12	-27	-20	-8	0	2	Σfx^1 −70				
$(fx^1)^2$	25	48	81	40	8	0	2	$\Sigma(fx^1)^2$ 204		Check		
Σfx^1y^1 −							1	Σfx^1y^1				
+	10	28	54	20	6	0		119				

$$r = \frac{\left\{\Sigma xy - \frac{\Sigma x \cdot \Sigma y}{N}\right\}}{\sqrt{\Sigma x^2 - \frac{(\Sigma x)^2}{N} \times \Sigma y^2 - \frac{(\Sigma y)^2}{N}}}$$

$$r = \frac{119 - \frac{(-70)(-39)}{46}}{\sqrt{204 - \frac{(-70)^2}{46} \times 99 - \frac{(-39)^2}{46}}}$$

$$= \frac{59.65}{\sqrt{(97.49)(65.94)}} = \frac{59.65}{\sqrt{6427.98}} = \frac{59.65}{80.18} = 0.75$$

$\Sigma xy = 119$

$\Sigma x = -70$

$\Sigma y = -39$

$N = 46$

$\Sigma x^2 = 204$

$\Sigma y^2 = 99$

r = 0.75

APPENDIX A(III - b)

SPLIT HALF RELIABILITY OF PSAT

Sl. No.	Odd	Even	Sum	Difference
1	16	9	25	7
2	23	25	48	-2
3	15	12	27	3
4	16	7	23	9
5	20	22	42	2
6	23	31	54	-8
7	16	19	35	-3
8	28	30	58	-2
9	8	7	15	1
10	14	20	34	-6
11	5	10	15	-5
12	10	7	17	7
13	30	27	57	3
14	18	20	38	-2
15	21	23	44	-2
16	28	23	51	5
17	29	26	55	3
18	26	26	52	0
19	17	15	32	2
20	15	13	28	2
21	18	24	42	-6
22	28	29	57	-1
23	27	20	47	7
24	26	31	57	-5
25	19	15	34	4
26	22	25	47	-3
27	32	32	64	0
28	25	24	49	1
29	13	10	23	3
30	30	24	54	6
31	18	20	38	-2

Sl. No.	Odd	Even	Sum	Difference
32	28	24	52	4
33	13	9	22	4
34	22	17	39	5
35	17	20	37	-3
36	28	29	57	-1
37	13	8	21	5
38	15	11	26	4
39	16	15	31	1
40	14	20	34	-6
41	17	21	38	-4
42	4	5	9	-1
43	18	24	42	-6
44	22	19	41	3
45	12	16	28	-4
46	26	30	56	-4
47	32	26	58	6
48	28	32	60	-4

Sum

Sum of 14 highest = 791

Sum of 14 lowest = 310

Difference D_s = 481

D_s^2 = 231361

Difference

Sum of 14 highest = 72

Sum of 14 lowest = -67

Difference D_D = 139

D_d^2 = 19321

$$r = 1 - \frac{D_d^2}{D_s^2} = 1 - \frac{19331}{231361} = 0.92$$

APPENDIX - A(IV)

PSAT SCORES AND TEACHER'S RATINGS FOR CONCURRENT VALIDITY

Sl. No.	PSAT Score	Teacher's ratings	Sl. No.	PSAT Score	Teacher's ratings
1	25	P*	26	47	P
2	48	G**	27	64	G
3	27	P	28	49	P
4	23	P	29	23	P
5	42	P	30	54	G
6	54	P	31	38	P
7	35	P	32	52	G
8	58	G	33	22	P
9	15	P	34	39	G
10	34	P	35	37	P
11	15	P*	36	57	G**
12	17	P	37	21	P
13	57	G	38	26	P
14	38	P	39	39	P
15	44	P	40	38	P
16	51	P	41	38	P
17	55	P	42	9	P
18	52	P	43	46	P
19	32	P	44	42	G
20	28	P	45	28	P
21	42	P	46	56	G
22	57	G	47	58	G
23	47	G	48	65	G
24	57	G	49	39	P
25	34	G	50	40	G

*P - Poor

** G - Good

APPENDIX - B(I)

Raw Scores Corresponding T-Scores and Composite T-Scores on SPM and THMAS

9th (B)

Sl. No.	Raw Scores		T-Scores		Composite T-Scores
	SPM	THMAS	SPM	THMAS	
1	51	14	61	52	113
2	48	11	58	45	103
3	49	13	59	50	109
4	50	13	60	50	110
5	47	17	57	60	117
6	36	18	47	62	109
7	50	13	60	50	110
8	41	16	52	57	109
9	51	16	61	57	118
10	38	21	49	70	119
11	43	17	53	60	113
12	52	16	62	57	119
13	44	12.5	54	48	102
14	46	11	56	45	101
15	15	11.5	28	46	74
16	13	12	27	47	74
17	34	17	45	60	105
18	40	20	51	67	118
19	37	6	48	32	80
20	41	14.5	52	53	105
21	36	18.5	47	63	110
22	37	13	48	50	98
23	45	18	52	62	114
24	35	7.5	46	36	82
25	14	9	28	40	68
26	29	13.5	41	51	92
27	43	18.5	53	63	116

Sl. No.	Raw Scores		T-Scores		Composite T-Scores
	SPM	THMAS	SPM	THMAS	
28	42	17.5	53	61	114
29	54	7	63	35	98
30	52	8	62	37	99
31	54	15	63	55	118
32	41	13	52	50	102
33	44	14.5	54	53	107
34	42	13	53	50	103
35	15	9.5	28	41	69
36	31	7	43	35	78
37	12	6.5	26	33	59
38	42	10.5	53	43	96
39	21	7	34	35	70
40	33	10	45	42	87
41	41	20	52	67	119
42	44	9.5	54	41	95
43	40	15	51	55	106
44	51	12	61	47	108
45	38	16	49	57	106
46	46	15	56	55	111
47	46	17	56	60	116
48	34	14	45	52	97
49	40	6	51	32	83
50	34	14	45	52	97
51	16	11.5	29	50	79
52	50	16.5	60	58	118
53	42	12	53	47	100

APPENDIX -B(II)

Raw Scores, Corresponding T-Scores and Composite T-Scores on SPM & THMAS

(9th C)

Sl. No.	Raw Scores		T-Scores		Composite T-Scores
	SPM	THMAS	SPM	THMAS	
1	14	15.5	13	49	62
2	27	14.5	29	45	74
3	44	16	51	51	102
4	44	17	52	55	107
5	42	16.5	49	53	102
6	48	18	57	59	116
7	26	16	28	51	79
8	47	16	56	51	107
9	47	19	56	64	120
10	46	20	54	68	122
11	48	17	57	55	112
12	48	16	57	51	108
13	52	19	62	64	126
14	52	17	62	55	117
15	49	16	58	51	109
16	48	14.5	57	45	102
17	41	14	47	42	89
18	31	10	35	25	60
19	50	16	60	51	111
20	49	15	58	47	105
21	50	16.5	60	53	113
22	38	15	44	47	91
23	48	17	57	55	112
24	32	20	36	68	104
25	45	19	53	64	117
26	45	14	53	42	95

Sl. No.	Raw Scores		T-Scores		Composite T-Scores
	SPM	THMAS	SPM	THMAS	
27	47	14	56	42	98
28	42	15	49	47	96
29	49	14	58	42	100
30	36	9	41	21	62
31	38	14.5	44	45	89
32	42	16.5	49	53	102
33	45	15.5	53	49	102
34	42	18	49	59	108
35	43	18	50	59	109
36	44	16.5	52	53	105
37	42	17	49	55	104
38	42	15	49	47	96
39	45	20	53	68	121
40	47	15	56	47	103
41	40	17	46	55	101
42	42	17	49	55	104
43	55	12	66	34	100
44	39	13	45	38	83
45	42	16	49	51	100
46	35	17	40	55	95

APPENDIX -B(III)

Matched Pairs Selected and Their Composite T- Scores

Sl. No.	IX 'B' Name	Composite T-Scores	IX 'C' Name	Composite T-Scores
1	B. Srinivas	119	N. Ashwini	120
2	G. Someshwara Bandari	118	C. Naresh	117
3	V.J. Smitha	117	Nayak Vinutha	117
4	V. G. Murali	116	K. Pavithra	116
5	B. Nivedita	113	R. Swetha	113
6	Iram Ahmed	113	B.U.Chaitanya	112
7	R. Nitin	111	P. Deepthi	111
8	B.G. Chaithra	109	M . Pallavi	109
9	Kushal.D. Shaw	109	V.A. Ajay Kumar	109
10	R. Narayan Raju	109	S. L. Ravindra	108
11	V. Purnima	108	S. Sunil	108
12	Mannan Shaikh	107	Chaithra R. Gupta	107
13	J. Kiran Kumar	106	T.M. Shilpa	107
14	M. Usha Jain	105	K. Ramya	105
15	B. Bharath	105	C. E. Vinutha	105
16	K.A. Sulochana	103	H. V. Ravikiran	103
17	N. Mahesh	102	B.H. Divya	102
18	Neha Maloo	102	R. Shriyanka	102
19	Isha	101	N. Seema	101
20	K.R. Sridevi	100	D. Sharath Manjithaya	100
21	Shabbir	99	G. Ramya	100
22	C. K. Rashmi	98	K.R. Shruthi	98
23	K.S. Kavitha	97	K.H. Srinivas	96
24	G.Sagar Pawar	96	S.A. Bhavani	96
25	A. Mohan Raj	95	P. Shilpa	95
26	M. Satish	92	K. Ramya	91
27	B.S. Charan	83	R. Deepa	83
28	B. R. Prathibha	79	G. Hamsa	79
29	K. Komal	74	B. Shivshankar	74
30	A. Manjula	59	P.S. Kannan	60

APPENDIX - C(I)

Topics adopted for Synectics Model of Teaching Science

Physics

- Optical Instruments - Camera
- Our Earth
- Volcano
- Motion
- Scalars
- Vectors
- Force
- Gravitation
- Magnetism

Chemistry

- Structure of atom (Rutherford's model)
- Kinetic theory of gases
- Covalent Bonding
- Ionic Bonding
- Modern Periodic Table
- Metals
- Ozone
- Recycling

Biology

- Parts of Human body and their functions
- Digestive system in man

- Heart
- Levels of organisation in living organisms
- Mitosis
- Meiosis
- Water cycle
- Water pollution

APPENDIX - C(II)

Planning Guide of Synectics Model of Teaching

(Making strange familiar)

I. Topic and Mode of Expression

1. Identify and describe briefly the topic
2. What mode of expression do the students use.

II. Educational Objectives

List the objectives the students accomplish after this lesson

III Planning for Direct Analogies

Suggest the direct analogies for the new material i.e. identify the new material with a person, plant , animal, situation or non living thing.

IV. Phases of the Model

Write the instructions and opening move for each phase of the model.

Phase One :	Substantive Input
	Provide information on new topic.
Phase Two :	Direct Analogy
	Suggest direct analogy and ask students to describe the analogy.
Phase Three :	Personal Analogy
	Get students to "become" the direct analogy.
Phase Four :	Comparing Analogies
	Students identify and explain the points of

	similarity between the new material and the direct analogy.
Phase Five :	Explaining Differences
	Students explain where the analogy doesn't fit.
Phase Six :	Exploration
	Students re-explore the original topic on its own terms.
Phase Seven :	Generating Analogy
	Students provide their own direct analogy and explore the similarities and differences.

APPENDIX - C(III)

Sample Lesson plans of Synectics Model of Teaching

Lesson Plan : 1

Subject: Chemistry

Topic : Structure of atom(Rutherford's model)

Description of the topic :

An atom is no more regarded as indivisible particle. It can be divided. Atom consists of three fundamental particles - protons, neutrons and electrons. Protons are positively charged, electrons are negatively charged and neutrons are neutral. Protons and neutrons constitute the nucleus. The nucleus is positively charged. The electrons revolve around the nucleus in an orbit. If the electrons are stationery they would be pulled into the nucleus. As they are in motion, which counter acts the pull of the nucleus they remain in their orbits.

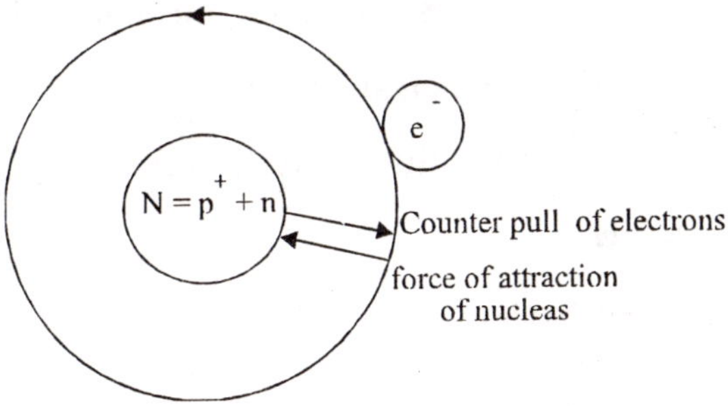

Mode of expression of students :

- Writing in worksheets provided
- Verbal interchange among themselves and with the teacher

Educational Objectives :

- Student is able to understand the structure of atom

- Student is able to empathise himself with the solar system
- Student is able to play with analogies
- Student is able to identify differences between the structure of atom and the solar system.
- Student is able to identify similarities between the structure of atom and the solar system.
- Student is able to identify differences between the structure of atom and the solar system.
- Student is able to describe the structure of atom.
- Student is able of draw the structure of atom.
- Student is able to suggest his own analogy to structure of atom.
- Student is able to identify similarities and difference between the structure of atom and his own analogy.
- Student develops creative ability.
- Student develops the ability to solve problems.

Direct Analogies:

- The solar System
- Bee hive
- A politician/ film star and his supporters
- Spider web
- A man spinning balls tied to threads of different lengths
- Dog and the bone game
- Game of cricket

- Merry-go round
- Earth and the moon(satellites)
- Fan

Phases of the model:

T :	As you know there are many objects on this earth. What do you think is the smallest thing or particle ?	Teacher introduces the topic to the class
S:	Mud grains, dust particles, powder etc.	Students gives examples for smallest particles
T:	Now let me take this chalk piece and start breaking it into pieces. As I go on doing this I get a small piece which I cannot break further. Even this small piece is made up of many minute particles called atom. Can these atoms be divided further ? What are these atoms made up of ? What is its structure? We need to answer these questions. We will study about the Rutherford's model of atom.	
		Phase I:
T:	Rutherford suggested a model for the structure of the atom. This is called the Rutherford's model. According to him, A atom is not an indivisible particle, it can be divided. Atom consists of three fundamental particles - protons, neutrons and electrons. Protons are positively charged, electrons are negattvely charged and neutrons are neutral	Substantive input Teacher provides information on the new topic-structure of atom Teacher records the charge of particles on the black board
	I will draw the structure of atom to show you the position or arrangement of these fundamental particles in an atom.	Teacher draws a diagram of an atom on the black board. Students observe the figure
	The protons and neutrons constitute the nucleus which is at the centre.	

	O.K. if the nucleus is made up of protons and neutrons would the nucleus be electrically charged?	
S :	Yes	
T:	What charge do you think the nucleus would have?	
S:	The nucleus would have a positive charge	Hypothesize that the nucleus has the positive charge
T:	Why would the nucleus have a positive charge?	
S:	Because the nucleus has protons and neutrons, the neutrons donot have any charge and the protons have positive charge. Hence the nucleus will be positively charged.	Students reasons out why the nucleus is positively charged
T:	You are right. The nucleus is at the centre of the atom and is positively charged. The electrons revolve around the nucleus in an orbit. But when the nucleus is positively charged and the electrons is negatively charged, don't you think it should be attracted and pulled into the nucleus? How will it remain in the orbit?	
S:	This can happen because the electrons are in motion, revolving around the nucleus in an orbit.	Students hypothesize that electrons move around the nucleus and hence they are not pulled inside.
T:	Yes, if the electrons were stationery they would be pulled into the nucleus. As they are in motion, they remain in the orbit. But how will their revolving motion help them to remain in the orbit?	
S:	As the electrons revolve they oppose the attractive pull of the nucleus	Students analyses that the motion opposes the attractive pull.

T:	Yes, As they are in motion, which counteracts the pull of the nucleus, they remain in their orbits	
T:	Now I will give you a worksheet. In the first page the description of structure of atom is given with the figure. Just go through it once with me as I read it out. If you have any doubts you can ask me.	Teacher provides the students with Synectics worksheets. Students follow the teacher as she reads the description and get their doubts clarified if any. **Phase 2:**
T:	Now you know something about the structure of the atom. The next thing we want to do is compare. I want you to think of the solar system. How is the solar system for comparison with structure of atom ? Can you do it?	**Direct analogy :** Teacher suggests Direct Analogy and asks students to describe the analogy
S:	Yes	
T:	Let us first describe the solar system. In the worksheet provided, you can describe whatever you know about the solar system in the second step.	
S:	Describe the solar system.	Students describes the solar system. One student from each group reads out their description.
T:	Let us share what each group has written . Now read out what you have written one by one.	Teacher records the relevant important points as students describe the solar system on the board.
S_1: S_2 S_3 S_4 S_5 S_6	Our solar system consist of the sun, plants and their satellites. The sun is at the centre with plants, asteroid and satellites revolving around the sun. There are nine planets revolving the sun in fixed orbit. The sun holds all the other members of the system bound to it by its (attractive) gravitational force.	

T:	What would happen if planets would be stationary	
S:	If the planets were stationery they would be pulled into the sun. As they are in motion which counteracts the pull of the sun, they remain in their orbit.	
		Phase 3:
T:	OK now you all agree with the description of the solar system. What I want you to do now is to be the solar system or a part of it like the sun or the planets. What are you now?	**Personal Analogy** Teacher has students 'become' the direct analogy i.e. the solar system.
S:	I am the sun	Student emphathizes himself with sun. Teacher directs them to write it down in the worksheet. Student records this in step 3 of the worksheet.
T:	How would you look like? Readout what you have written	Teacher asks the student to state from a personal frame of reference. Student writes it down in the worksheet
S_1:	I am spherical in shape	Teachers records their contributions.
S_2	I am red and burning.	
S_3	I am hot	
S_4	I am a fire ball	
S_5	I have so many planets revolving around me	
S_6	I am in the centre of the solar system	
T:	OK What would you be doing being the sun.	Teacher directs the personal analogy to a kinesthetic perspective

S:	I keep burning I pull the planets towards me by my gravitational force	Student writes it down in the worksheet and then shares it with the other groups.
T:	How would you feel being the sun?	Teachers directs the personal analogy to the emotional perspective Teacher records students responses.
S:	I feel important	
T:	How would you feel important?	Teacher asks for the justification
S:	I feel so important because I am at the centre and have 9 planets revolving around me. I am happy. I feel proud that planets revolve round me. I am proud that I control all the planets by my gravitational force.	Students describe what they perceive being the sun is like.
S:	I am proud of my family of planets. I am the boss of the solar system. I am sad that I cannot go near my family members because they will be burnt if they come near me. I feel sad that I may be burnt out after many years.	Teacher records all the responses.
		Phase 4:
T :	Now we have a good list of how would it be if you were the sun in the solar system. Now I want you to list down the connections you see between description of structure of atom and the solar system. Certain elements related to the solar system are given in step 4 of your worksheet. Against each of the elements write down the elements related to structure of atom which you think are parallel.	**Comparing Analogies** Teacher asks the students to identify and explain the points of simlarity between structure of atom and the solar system.

S:	Sun → Nucleus (Protons and Neutrons) H atoms → Neutrons Planets → electrons Orbit of planets → orbit of electron Gravitational force → Attractive force revolution of planets → revolution of electrons round the sun → round the nucleus Planets remain in orbit as its motion counteracts the sun's pull → electrons remain in orbit as its motion counteracts the pull of nucleus	Student identifies the parallel elements of structure of atom. Teacher records it on the Black board.
T:	You have compared the elements of the solar system with that of the structure of atom. The drawing of the structure of atom given in first page of your worksheet is exactly copied here in the 4th step. Use what you have discovered about the similarities between structure of atom and solar system to label this drawing in terms of the solar system. Be sure that you write something in each box. OK. Now go on.	
S:	Label the different parts in terms of the solar system	Student labels the different parts of the figure in terms of the solar system
T:	Now write a short paragraph showing your analogical connections	Student explains the analogical connections
S:	Writes	
T:	Let us share what you have written one by one.	
S_1: S_2	As the sun is the centre of the solar system, the nucleus is at the centre of the atom. The sun is made up of	

S_3 S_4 S_5 S_6	hydrogen and the nucleus is made up of protons and neutrons. As the planets revolve round the sun in a fixed orbit, similarly the electrons revolve round the nucleus in a fixed orbit. The sun attracts the planets towards it by gravitational force similarly the nucleus attracts the electrons by electrical attractive force. Because of their motion/ revolution the planets counteract the pull of the sun, and remain in the orbit. Similarly the electrons revolve round the atom and are never stationery and hence this motion counteracts the pull of the nucleus.	
		Phase 5:
T:	We have seen the similarities between structure of atom and the solar system. You might think the atom is quite unlike our solar system. We will look for the differences between an atom and the solar system. Now list down the differences in your worksheet.	**Explaining differences** Students explain where the analogy of the solar system doesnot fit.
S″	The solar system is huge and the structure of the atom is small. There are 9 planets in the solar system and all have different sizes, but all the electrons have the same size. The electrons are electrically charged particles. But the planets and sun are not charged. The nucleus has positive charge and attracts the electrons which are negatively charged due to its electrical attractive force. But the sun attracts the planets by its gravitational force. Hence the solar system is bound by gravitational force but electrons are held to nucleus due to attractive force.	
		Phase 6:
T:	Yes. By now you all have an idea about the structure of atom. Now write down a short paragraph of your own on the structure of atom in step 7 in your worksheet.	**Exploration**
S:	Describe the structure of atom in their own words and write it down in the worksheet	Student explore the structure of atom in its own terms.

T:	Now let us listen to how all the groups have described the structure of atom we will start reading it out group by group. OK.	Student reads the description and others listen.
		Phase 7:
T:	Very good. Now you clearly know the structure of atom. We will again play with some analogies to the structure of atom. This time you will suggest the analogy. What in the world is like the structure of atom and could be compared to it.	**Generating Analogy** Teacher moves the students into analogies by asking for a direct analogy
S_1:	Suggests different analogies like	Students provide their own direct analogy
S_2	A film star with his supporters	Teacher records students contributions
S_3	Dog and the bone game........	
S_4		
S_5		
S_6		
T:	Describe how your example is similar to the structure of atom and record it in your worksheet	Teacher asks for an explanation of the suggested analogy.
S:	Lists the similarities between their analogy and the structure of atom and records it	Students explore the similarities
T:	OK you may feel analogue is quite unlike the structure of atom.	
T:	Yes write down how your analogue is different from structure of atom	
S:	Lists down the differences between structure of atom and his analogue and explains where the analogue doesnot fit.	Students explore the differences between their analogue and structure of atom.
T:	Let us share what similarities and differences each group has found to their own analogue.	
S:	Read out how the analogue is similar to structure of atom and where their analogue does not fit.	
T:	OK Very good. Now we have enjoyed playing with analogies and we also studied the structure of atom. You have given good analogies and described the structure of atom	Teacher concludes the lesson by praising the students.

beautifully. This is the end of our lesson and I want to thank all of you. You were really terrific.

Lesson Plan : 2

Subject : Physics

Topic : Camera

Description of Topic :

Camera structure and its working mechanism: The most important part of the camera is the lens. It is a convex lens. This lens forms a real, inverted, diminished image of a distant object at the principal focus of the lens. The lens is normally closed by a shutter. When the camera is clicked, lens and the film gets exposed to light for a fraction of a second and an image is formed on the film.

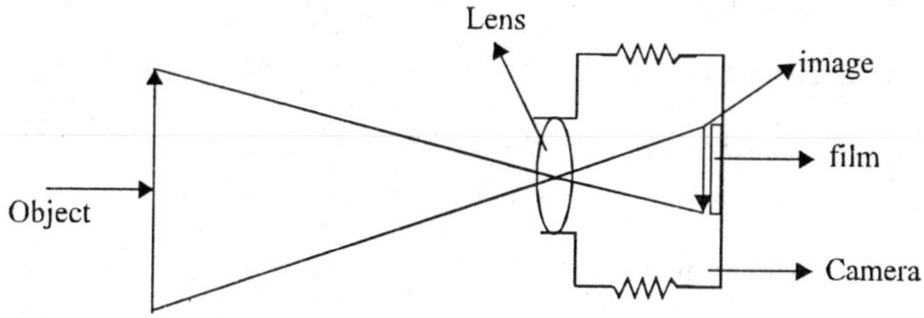

Mode of expression to students.:

- Verbal interchange among themselves and with the teacher.
- Writing and drawing figures in worksheet provided.

Educational objectives:

- Student is able to understand the making of a camera.
- Student is able to identify the parts of a camera.
- Student is able to understand the working mechanism of a camera

- Student is able to play with analogies
- Student is able to explain the structure and function of human eye.
- Student is able to empathize himself with the human eye
- Student is able to identify the similarities between a camera and human eye
- Student is able to identify the differences between a camera and human eye
- Student is able to describe the making and working mechanism of a camera.
- Student is able to draw a sketch of the image formation in a camera.
- Student is able to suggest his own analogy for camera.
- Student is able to identify similarities and differences between his own analogy and a camera
- Student develops the ability to solve problems.
- Student develops creative ability.

Direct Analogies

Human eye
Window
Prison Cell
Computer
House

Phases of the model

T:	Whenever you go to a picnic or whenever you have a function, you would all like to capture those happy moments and keep watching	Teacher introduces the topic to the class

	it whenever you want. Isn't it. What would you do for that.	
S:	Yes. We would take the photos	
T:	To take these photos you need an instrument. What is it?	
S:	The Camera	Student recalls the camera.
T:	Do you know how the camera works and how it is made?	
S:	No maa'm.	
T:	Today we will see how a camera works and the important parts of it. OK	
S:	Yes	
		Phase 2:
T:	You all know the camera is used to click photos. Is it enough if you just take a camera. Don't you need to buy something else whenever you want to take photos? What is it?	**Substantive input** Teacher provides information on the working of a camera.
S:	We need to buy a film	
T:	Yes a film is needed. What else do you know about a camera?	
S:	It has a lens	Student recalls the parts of a camera.
T:	Yes the most important part of the camera is the lens. It is a convex lens. This lens forms a real, inverted, diminished image of a distant object at its principal focus. You take a photograph of your mother, is the photo as big as her.	Teacher draws the diagram of a camera and schematically represents image formation.
S:	No . It is small	
T:	The image is diminished and inverted.	Student recognizes that the image is diminished.

T:	Can you guess at what distance is the film fixed in the camera?	
S:	A film is fixed at the principal focus of the lens.	Student guesses that film has to be fixed at principal focus of the lens
T:	Why?	
S:	It is because the image is formed at the principal focus of the lens	Student hypothesis that it is because image is formed at the principal focus.
T:	Is the lens always open?	
S:	No.	
T:	The lens is normally closed by a shutter. When the camera is clicked, the lens and the film gets exposed for a fraction of a second and an image is formed on the film.	
T:	Now you have understood how a camera works. I will give you the worksheet. In the first page the working mechanism of camera is given. Just go through it once as I read it out. If you have any doubts you can ask me.	Teacher provides the students with Synectics worksheets.
S:	OK Maa'm	Student follows the teacher as she reads the description and get their doubts clarified if any.-
		Phase 2:
T:	Is it clear. Now you know how a camera works. Now we will compare the camera to a human eye. You all know how the human eye works. In the worksheet write down whatever you know about the eye in the second step.	**Direct analogy** Teacher suggests direct analogy and asks students to describe the analogy
T:	What is the shape of the human eye?	

S:	Spherical. It is like a hollow ball. The eye lens is convex. It is made up of organic material	Student recalls the shape of eye. Student describes the structure of human eye.
T:	Where is the image formed?	
S:	On the retina.	Student recalls that image is formed on the retina.
T:	It acts as a screen for formation of the image. The pupil is the opening through which light enters the eye. The retina acts as a screen on which real, inverted image of the object is formed.	
T:	Let us share what each group has written. Now read out what you have written one by one.	
S_1 S_2 S_3 S_4 S_5 S_6	Reads out the description written on the human eye	Teacher records the important points as students describe the human eye.
		Phase 3:
T:	OK Now you all know how an image is formed in the human eye. Now I want you all to be the human eye. What are you?	**Personal Analogy** Teacher has students become the direct analogy, the human eye.
S:	The human eye	Student empathises himself with the human eye
T:	Write down in your worksheets what you are? How would you look like and how would you feel? Now read out what you have written in?	Student records in the worksheet

T:	How would you look like?	
S_1	I am spherical	
S_2	I am hollow inside	
S_3	I have a pupil, convex lens, eyelid,	
S_4	and a retina	
S_5	My pupil can be black, blue, brown.	
S_6		
T:	What would you be doing being the eye?	Teacher directs the Personal analogy to a kinesthetic perspective
S:	I keep watching. I can see things around me/in the world I am a sense organ I am very sensitive to dust, when people cut onion and when sad I shed tears	
T:	How would you feel being the human eye?	Teacher directs the personal analogy to an emotional perspective.
S:	I feel so important because everybody needs me to see the world. I feel proud .	
T:	Why would you feel proud?.	Teacher asks for justification
S:	Because it is only because of me human beings can see the beautiful nature.	Student describes what they perceive being the human eye is like.
S_1 S_2 S_3 S_4 S_5 S_6	I feel guilty because if I am not able to work the human beings blind unable to see I like spectacles. They are my best friend because when I donot function properly they help me. I enjoy seeing beautiful things around.	Teacher records the responses

	I am glad that it is because of me people get attracted to each other I feel sad that when people are old, I become tired and loose my ability to function properly after many years of working.	
		Phase 4:
T:	Now we have a good list of how would you feel if you were the human eye. Now I want you to list down the connections you see between descritpion of camera and the human eye. Certain elements related the human eye are given in step 4 of your worksheet. Against each of the elements write down the elements related to camera which are parallel.	**Comparing analogies** Teacher asks the students to identify and explain the points of similarities between camera and human eye.
S:	Human eye → Camera - Convex lens → Convex lens - Retina → Film - Real, inverted, diminished image → Real, inverted, diminished image	Student identifies the similar elements in a camera
T:	You have compared the elements of human eye with the camera. The drawing of camera given in first page of your worksheet is exactly copied here in the 4th step. Use what you have discovered about the similarities between camera and human eye to label this drawing in terms of the human eye. Be sure you write something in every box. OK Now start.	Teacher records the responses on Black board.
S:	Labels	Student labels the figure of camera in terms of human eye.

T:	Now write a short paragraph showing your analogical connections between human eye and camera in step 5.	
S:	Writes	Student explains the analogical connections.
T:	Let us share what you have written. You can read it one by one. One of you in each group can present it.	
S_1 S_2 S_3 S_4 S_5 S_6	The lens of a camera is convex just like the one in the human eye. The retina is the screen on which the image is formed in the eye similarly the film is the screen on which the image is formed in the camera. The image formed is real, inverted and diminished in both the eye and the camera. The image is formed at the principal focus of the lens and the retina and the film are fined at the principal focus.	
		Phase 5:
T:	We have seen the similarities between camera and human eye. You might think that an eye is quite unlike a camera. We will look for the difference between camera and human eye. Now list down where you feel the human eye is different from a camera in your worksheet.	**Explaining differences** Teacher asks students to identify where the analogy, eye doesnot fit.
S:	In human eye the lens is made up of organic material but in a camera a lens is of inorganic material An eye cannot be manufactured by man but a camera can be	Student explains the differences between eye and camera.
		Phase 6:
T:	Yes. By now you all have an idea about the working mechanism of a camera. Now write down a short paragraph of your own on the	**Exploration**

	camera in step 7 in your worksheet.	
S:	Explain the working of a camera in their own words in their worksheet	
T:	Let us listen to what all the groups have written about a camera. Start reading it group by group.	Student explores the working mechanism of camera in its own terms.
		Phase 7
T:	Excellent. Now you all know the working mechanism of a camera. We will again play with some analogies to a camera. Now you suggest the analogy. What in the world would be compared to a camera.	**Generating analogy** Teacher moves the students to analogies by asking for direct analogy
S:	Write it down in worksheet step 8 suggests different analogies Prison cell Computer etc.	Student provides their own Direct Analogy to a camera.
T:	Describe how your analyze is similar to a camera and record it in your worksheet	
S:	Lists similarities between their analogy and a camera	Student explores the similarities between camera and their analogy.
T:	Next explain where your analogue does not fit and how it is different from a camera.	
S:	Explains the differences between camera and their analogue	Student explores the difference between camera and their analogy.
T:	We all would like to know about analogy selected by each group. You can read it out one by one. OK. The first group can read it out first.	
S:	Read out how their analogue is similar and is different from a camera.	

T:	Yes. Wonderful students. We have all enjoyed playing with analogies and simultaneously we have also come to know the working mechanism of a camera. All the analogies were good. This is the end of our less and thank you.	Teacher concludes the lesson by praising the students.

Lesson Plan : 3

Subject : Biology

Topic : Cell division : Mitosis

Description of the topic :

Mitosis :

It is the most common type of cell division occurring in higher plants and animals. During mitosis parent cell divides into two daughter cells, each with the same number of chromosomes as found in the parent cell. Therefore mitosis is also called equation division. A number of important changes take place in the cell once division is initiated. These changes can be studied under four phases: Prophase, Metaphase, Anaphase and Telophase.

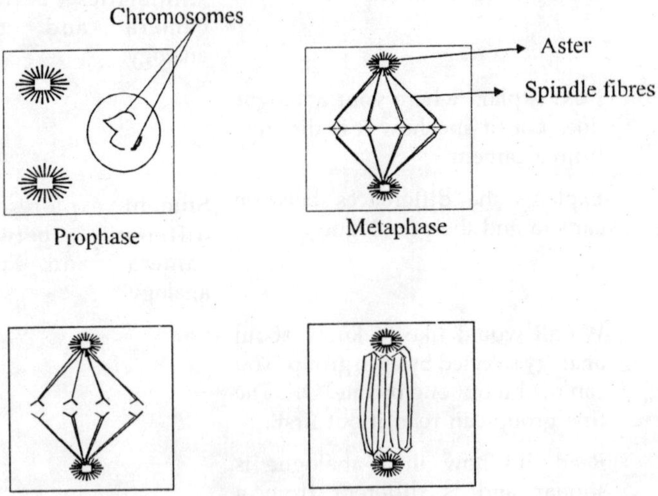

Anaphase

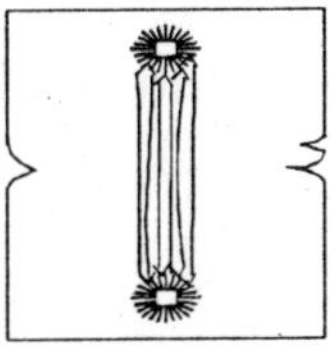

Telophase

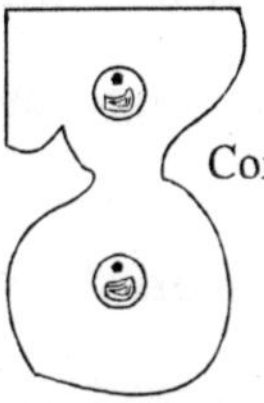

Cytokenesis

Prophase :

At this stage chromatin network breaks and the threads become more distinct, short and thick. They are now called chromosomes. Each chromosome appears to be made of 2 parallel strand held together to a point called centromere. The nucleus and nuclear membrane disappear and thus the chromosomes are set free in the cytoplasm.

Metaphase :

During this phase the chromosomes moves towards the centrę and arrange along the equatorial plane.

Anaphase :

The spindel fibers pull the centromere towards their respective poles. The centromere divides into 2 and the two chromatids repel and begin to move away to opposite poles.

Telophase :

It is the final phase where a daughter nuclear is formed at each pole. A nucleolus is organized and a nuclear membrane is formed around each set of chromosomes resulting in the formation of two identical daughter nuclei.

Simultaneously the cell starts dividing into two and a cell wall appears between each cell in plants and clevary furrow in case of animals. Thus one parent cell is divided into 2 identical daughter cells. Mitosis is essential for growth, healing of wounds etc.

Mode of expression of students :

- verbal interchange among themselves and with the teacher
- Writing in worksheets provided
- Drawing figures.

Educational objectives:

- Student identifies the need for mitosis
- Student appreciates the process of mitosis
- Student plays with analogies
- Student explains what happens before during and after the parition of a country.
- Student analogises between the partition of a country and mitosis.
- Student identifies the similarities between partition of a country and mitosis.
- Student identifies the differences between partition of a country and mitosis.
- Student explains the process of mitosis cell division
- Student identifies the phases of mitotic cell division.
- Student describes the different changes occurring in the different phases.
- Student suggests his own analogy for mitosis.
- Student states similarities and differences between his own analogy and mitosis
- Student develops ability to solve problems.
- Student develops creative ability is fostered.

Direct analogies :

Partition of a country.
Tug of war.
Division of a political party.
Partition in a house.
Preparation of jammons/chapathis from a mass of dough.
Nuclear fission.
Mercury.

Phases of the model:

T:	You have a cut or a wound on your body. It heals after some time. Isn't it . How does it heal?	Teacher introduces the topic to the class
S:	The skin grows again on this wound.	Student recalls that the skin grows.
T:	How does this skin grow.	
S:	No response	
T:	The skin has many cells. Isn't it. The cells start dividing and grow in number. This process where cells increase in number by dividing is called cell division. Do you know how these cells divide.	
S:	No	
T:	Today let us study about cell division OK	
		Phase 1:
T:	There are two types of cell division a) Mitosis and 2) Meosis. It is the most common type of cell division. It occurs in higher plants and animals. During mitosis parent cell divides into two daughter cells, each with the same number of chromosomes as found in the parent cell. Can you guess what this division is also called because of this result.	**Substantive Input** Teacher provides information on the new topic - Mitotic cell division.

S:	Equal division	Student guesses that it is called equal division
T:	Mitosis is also called equation division. A number of important changes take place in the cell once division is initiated. These changes can be studied under four phases: Prophase, Metaphase, Anaphase and Telophase. Let us see what happens during the 4 phases. The first is the prophase	Teacher displays a chart of the four phases.
T:	In the prophase the chromatin network breaks and the threads become more distinct, short and thick. They are now called chromosomes. Each chromosome appears to be made of 2 parallel strands held together to a point called centromere. The nucleus and nuclear membrane disappear. What would happen if nucleus membrane disappears ?	Student observes the figure in the chart.
S:	The chromosomes are free in the cytoplasm	Student guesses that chromosomes might be free in the cytoplasm.
T:	Yes now the chromosomes are set free in the cytoplasm.	
T:	Now we go on to the metaphase. In this phase the chromosomes moves towards the centre and arrange along the equatorial plane. Which is the next phase?	
S:	Anaphase	Student recalls the third phase of mitosis.
T:	In the third phase i.e. the anaphase the centromere divides into 2 and the 2 chromatids repel and begin to	

	move away to opposite poles. The spindel fibers pull the centromeres towards their respective poles.	
T:	In the fourth and final stage i.e. the Telophase, a daughter nucleus is formed at each pole. A nucleolus is orgnaised and a nuclear membrane is formed around each set of chromosomes, resulting in the formation of two identical daughter nuclei. Simultaneously the cell starts dividing into 2 and a cell wall appears between each cell in plants and in case of animals the clevary furrow appears. Thus one parent cell is divided into 2 identical daughter cells. One thing you should know here is these phases are not distinct and the changes occur continuously. Mitosis is essential for growth, healing of wound etc.	
T:	Now you know how mitotic cell division occurs.	
T:	What are the four phases and what are the changes that occur during each of the phases?	Student names the four phases Student describes the changes occurring during each phase.
T:	You are provided with a work sheet. In the first page the process of mitosis is described. Let us go through it once. Just look into the description as your friend reads it out. If you have any doubts you can stop and ask me.	Teacher provides the students with Synectics worksheets.
S:	Reads the paragraph on mitosis.	Student follows as one student reads the paragraph and get their doubts clarified if any.

T:	In the last class we had studied about cells. To what did we compare a cell to?	
S:	To a country.	Student recalls that cell was compared to a country.
T:	Then to what could cell division be compared to?	
S:	To partition of a country?	Student guesses the analogy
T:	Yes, Think of what happens in a country, before, during and after partition and write it down in your worksheet. You can compare the parts of a cell to parts of a government as we did in the last class. Can you do it?	
S:	Yes.	Student explains incidents occurring during partition.
T:	Let us share what each group has written. One of you from each group can read out what you have written one by one.	
S_1 S_2 S_3 S_4 S_5 S_6	Before the people of different groups live harmoniously sharing some land, Government etc. with friendship together. Some disturbance sets and the enemity develops. The enemity makes them to have 2 different lands for each side. The people of different groups divide into two. They dislike each other and move away from each other to 2 different lands. The land is divided and 2 different governments are formed and two different countries emerge. Each country will have a different governing system, different	One student from each group reads out their incidents listed.

	transportation system etc. Thus one country is divided into two.	
		Phase 3:
T:	OK Now I want you to become the country which is divided ? OK What are you?	Personal Analogy Teacher has students 'become' the direct analogy i.e. the country.
S:	I am a country	Student empathizes himself.
T:	How would you be if you were the country?	Teacher asks the students to state from a personal frame of reference how they look. Teacher directs them to write it down in the worksheet.
S:	I have a boundary. I have my own land, mountains, rivers, forests, cities, beautiful people living together . They will be proud to be my citizen. I am beautiful.	Student records in step 3 of the work sheet.
T:	What would happen if there is a partition?	Teacher directs the Personal analogy to a kinesthetic perspective.
S:	My land is divided into two different boundaries between the 2 are marked. The mountain, forests are all divided. Enmity will develop between them. Different groups will move to different sides dividing everything.	
T:	How would you feel being the country?	Teacher directs the Personal analogy to an emotional perspective.
S:	I am proud to be a country .	
T:	Why are you proud?	Teacher asks for a justification

S_1 S_2 S_3 S_4 S_5 S_6

I am proud to have all the mountains, rivers and beautiful forests in me.

I am happy that other people like my beauty.

I am proud to have a beautiful shape/boundary .....

T: How would you feel if there is a partition.?

S_1 S_2 S_3 S_4 S_5 S_6

I would feel sad that all my parts are divided

I would be happy because I will have 2 names .

I will become two. I will have 2 new different governing systems, polices, different transportation, communication network etc.

Student describes what they perceive being the country under partition is like.

Teacher records the responses.

Phase 4:

Comparing analogies:

Teacher asks the students to identify and explain the points of similarity between partition of a country and mitosis.

T: Now we have a good list of how would it be if you were a country and there was a partition. Now I want you to list down the connections you see between mitosis and partition of a country. Certain elements related to partition of a country is given in step 4 of your worksheet. Against each of the elements write down the elements related to mitosis which you think are parallel.

Country → Cell

Before partition → Before cell division

Partition → Mitosis

Initial stage of partition → Prophase

Government → Nucleus

2nd Stage of partition → Metaphase

Student identifies the similar elements of mitosis

Teacher records it on the Black board.

3rd Stage of partition → Anaphase

The people hate other group → Repulsion of centromeres

Move towards 2 lands → move towards 2 poles

Enemity - Spindel fibers

Final stage → Telophase

2 boundaries arise → cell wall/ Calvary furrow

2 countries are formed with different governments → 2 daughter cells are formed with different nucleus.

T:	You have compared the elements of parititon of the country with that of mitosis. Now write a short paragraph showing your analogical connections	Student explains the analogical connections.
S:	Write down on the worksheet where the analogy fits.	
T:	Now read out the paragraph one by one.	
S_1 S_2 S_3 S_4 S_5 S_6	As the country before partition is one, the cell is also one before division. The mitosis cell division process is equal to the process of partition of country. The prophase is the first stage where chromosomes appear, the nucleus and nuclear membrane disappear. Similarly in the initial stage of partition the network between people breaks and the government is dissolved. In the second phase i.e. the metaphase, the chromosomes move towards the centre and arrange along an equatorial plane.	Student explains the analogical connections

In the anaphase, the spindel fibers pull the centromere towards their respective poles. The centromere divides into 2 and the two chromatids repel and begin to move away to opposite poles as it happens in the III stage of partition i.e. the feeling of hatred pulls the people towards different lands. The group of people divide into 2 and they repel each other and begin to move to opposite sides. As in the final stage of mitosis, Telophase where 2 daughter nuclei are formed at each pole. 2 countries are formed from a single country in partition.

As in the cell, a nucleolus is organized and a nuclear membrane is formed around each set of chromosomes, similarly a different government is formed and a boundary between the two groups of people is framed.

Phase 5:

Explaining differences :

T: We have seen the similarities between partition of a country and mitosis. You might think the process of mitosis is unlike the partition of a country in some aspects. Now we will look for the differences between them. List them down in your worksheet.

Student explains where the analogy of the partition of country doesnot fit.

S: Mitosis is natural process whereas partition is man made. Mitosis is for the construction i.e. growth whereas partition causes destruction sometimes. Mitosis leads to division of one parent cell into 2 cells which are identical whereas partition of a country leads to unidentical 2 countries which are smaller. In mitosis all the phases go on continuously in the same order every

Student identifies the differences between mitosis and partition.

	time whereas in partition it may not be so.	
		Phase 6:
T:	Yes. By now you all know about Mitosis. Now write down a short paragraph of your own on Mitosis explaining with the help of figures.	**Exploration**
S:	Draw the figure of 4 phases of Mitosis and explain the process of Mitosis	Students re-explore the process of Mitosis in its own terms.
T:	Now let us see how all the groups have explained the process of Mitosis	
S:	Reads out the explanation of process of Mitosis.	
		Phase 7:
T:	Excellent. Now you clearly know about Mitosis. We will again play with analogies. This time you will suggest and choose the analogy for Mitosis. What in the world could be compared to Mitosis?	**Generating Analogy:** Teacher moves the students into analogies by asking for a direct analogy
S_1	Students suggests different analogies like:	Students provide their own direct analogy.
S_2	Division of a house	Teacher records students contribution.
S_3	Tug of war game	
S_4	Making jamoons from mass of dough	
S_5	Nuclear fission etc.	
T:	Describe how your analogue is similar to Mitosis and record it in your worksheet	Teacher asks for an explanation of the suggested analogy.
S:	Lists the similarities between their analogy and Mitosis	Students explore the similarities between their analogue and Mitosis.
T:	OK you may feel your analogue is quite unlike Mitosis . Write down how your analogue is different from Mitosis.	

S:	List down the differences between their analogy and Mitosis	Students explore where the analogy doesnot fit.
T:	Let us share what similarities and differences each group has found to their analogue.	
S:	Read out how their analogue is similar to and is different from Mitosis.	
T:	OK It was wonderful playing with analogies and we have also come to know about Mitosis. You have given good analogies and described Mitosis beautifully. We will end our lesson today. Thank you.	Teacher concludes the lesson by praising the students.

APPENDIX C(IV -a)

Sample of Stretching Exercise - Personal Analogy

A passenger train:

T: What would you be doing

S: 1) I would carry passenger from place to place.

2) I would be running a riles.

3) I eat fuels.

T: How would you feel?

S:

1) I am scared to run on bridges.

2) I is very tired

3) I feel dirty as I emit smoke

4) I would not be able to speak

5) She can go to place to place without wasting money.

6) I am happy that I make a noise which is likeable to children.

7) I am proud the only person who is having most number of wheels.

Being a cloud

T: What are you, what are you doing. How do you feel?

1) I am a cloud

2) I will bring rain.

3) I prevent the sun rays.

1) I will keep dashing.

2) I can see airplanes.

3) Sun will hide behind me.

4) Many people enjoy by seeing me.

5) I can move with wind.

6) I can be in many shape.

T: How do you feel being a cloud.

1) I enjoy

2) I love to be friendly with birds and planes.

1) I feel sad that I am dying very fast

2) I felt hot being near the sun.

3) I would be angry on the sun.

A Flower

T: What are you, what are you doing. How do you feel?

St 1) I give fragrance to others

St 2) I have different colours

St 3) I give nectar to Butterfly.

St 4) I am a symbol of love.

St 5) I am used for making perfume.

St 6) All the people admire me.

T: What do you feel?

St 1) I fell hurt when some body plucks me.

St 2) I fell proud because gods are decorated with me.

St 3) I think I am beautiful

St 4) I fell sad that my life is short.

St 5) I fell sad so that I have thorn.

Titanic ship

T: What would you be doing?

St 1) I carry people

St 2) I am sailing

St 3) I am getting lit by an ice berg.

St 4) I am huge

T: How would you feel?

St 1) I am sad as I am controlled by a master.

St 2) I feel proud that I am popular

St 3) I fell proud that my model is on a coke.

St 4) I am happy so that movie is done on me.

St 5) I can see water animals.

St 6) I am sad that I killed many movies.

Cockroach.

T: What wold you be doing?

St 1) I am moving on spoilt food.

St 2) I bit sarees.

St 3) I give rotten fragrance.

St 4) I frighten children.

T: How would you feel?

St 1) I am proud that I have 13 hearts.

St 2) I am proud that I live in all the houses.

St 3) Most of the people is fond of me.

St 4) I am proud that I have a long mustache.

St 5) I am scared that they will put poison.

St 6) I fell happy when I scare people.

APPENDIX C(IV -b)

Sample of stretching Exercise : Direct Analogy

How is your examination like a cricket match ?

Examination	A Cricket Match.
Student	——— Batsman
Paper setter	———Bowler
Questions	———Bal
Invigilator	———Umpire
Tough questions	———Fast Bowling
Tricky questions	———Spin Bowling
Objective type questions	——— Single run
Answering well	———Good batting
Very good marks (out of out)	———Century

Highest scorer	———Man of the match
Caught while coping	———Run out
Failed	———Bowled
Scored no marks	———duck
Finished Examination	———End of Innings.

APPENDIX - C(V)

Worksheet of a Synectics lesson

VOLCANO

1. You have seen volcanoes on T.V or in movies. When volcanoes burst and erupt they have known to have buried whole cities. What goes on inside to make them so violent/ What makes them blow up? To understand this just recall what you studied in the last class about the earth. In the previous class we studied that the earth is not a hard, solid ball of rock. Only the earth's crust is hard but inside, the earth is filled with magma which is hot, liquid rock.

The upper region of the earth's mantle just below the crust has molten rocks and gases called magma. The magma shifts about and pushes against the earth's crust from underneath. Magma can emerge out through vents (weak spots) on the earth's surface. Some times, a vent may have been plugged by natural process and this prevents the magma from emerging. As the gases accumulate underneath, they begin to exert tremendous pressures until the plug gives way. This results in a spectacular volcanic eruption with the red-hot lava spewing out through the vent and flows down rapidly and solidifies as it cools down. A schematic figure of a volcano erupting is shown below in the figure:

2. Let us think of something which is similar to a volcano. How is a cut on the human body. Let us take the analogy as the cut in the human body. Now describe what happens before and after there is a cut on the human body.

Before there is a cut on the skin, the blood is flowing inside.

The heart is pumping the blood with force and the blood is moving with force and will exert tremendous pressure on the vessels.

When the skin is cut the blood flows out due to high pressure inside the blood vessels.

3. Now imagine yourself to be the blood in the human body. Who are you? What would you look like?

I am the blood moving inside the skin of human body.

I am a liquid and my color is red.

4. What would you be doing?

I flow inside the skin. I am pumped by the heart to different parts of the human body. I move with much speed while moving. I exert pressure on the skin. I am confined to stay within the body by the skin. The only way I can come out is through a cut. I stop flowing after some time as I clot after I come out.

What would happen to you when there is a cut on the body?

I can come out through the cut and start flowing out. I stop flowing after some time as I clot after some time of coming out.

How would you feel?

I feel so important since life goes on because of me. I am happy that I provide nutrients and oxygen to all parts of the body.

- I am tired of moving always.
- I am sad because I can never stand in one place and take rest.

- I am always in tension and I exert pressure on the veins.

5. Now write a short paragraph showing your analogical connections between a volcano and a cut on a human skin.

- A volcano is like a cut in a human body.
- The skin is the outer surface of the human body and the blood flows inside it. Similarly the earth's crust is the outer surface of the earth and magma moves inside. The blood is in liquid form and the magma also. As the skin exerts pressure on skin like-wise magma pushes against the earth's crust.
- If there is a cut on the skin, the blood oozes out suddenly. Similarly if a vent gives way the volcano erupts.
- As the blood clots after some time the magma solidifies after sometime as it gets cooled.

6. You might think a volcano is quite unlike a bleeding cut on human body. What are the differences between a bleeding cut and a volcano?

- Volcano is a natural process but the cut on a human body is externally done by some object.
- The vent is a weak spot on the earth's crust and magma erupts through these vents. But cut on a human body does not occur in any weak spot of skin but cut can be cut anywhere.
- Volcano cannot be stopped. Blood flow can be stopped.
- Magma solidifies after it gets cooled. Blood gets clot because of some chemical reactions in blood. Magma is red because it is hot. Blood is red as haemoglobin is present in it.

- The vent gives way because of pressure exerted because of gases accumulating underneath. The cut is not because of blood exerting pressure but could be caused by some sharp object.

7. By now you have an idea about a volcano. Write down a short paragraph of your own on a volcano.

- Magma is made up of molten rocks and gases and is in liquid form. It is below the earth's crust. The magma keeps moving inside and exerts pressure on the earth's crust, There are some weak spots on the earth's crust called vents. Some natural process plugs these vents and magma cannot come out. But when gases accumulate they exert so much pressure that the vents get open and magma erupts with tremendous force and solidifies after cooling.

8. Find an example of your own. What in the world is like a volcano?

- A short tempered man. He boils with anger if he is tempted or disturbed.

9. Describe how your example acts like a volcano.

- Anger of man is like magma. Anger is kept inside his mind just like the magma is present below the earth's crust. In some weak situation man explodes with anger just like weak spots on earth giving way to magma to come out. If he suppresses his anger he will suddenly burst out in some weak situation just like the magma which exerts pressure and erupts through weak spots in the earth. Just as a man controlling anger the magma is also held inside the earth's crust. In anger he may destroy things or cause pain to some one just like the volcano destroys things when it comes out. Anger cools down after some time and the volcano also cools down and solidifies after some time.

10. How is your analogue different from a volcano?

   - Anger is a state of mind of humans but magma is a natural thing or matter. Anger can be controlled or cooled down if man wants but volcano cannot be stopped by man. After anger is cooled we cannot know it was there but when lava is cooled it solidifies.

Bibliography

Agarwal, Y.P., *Statistical Methods,* Sterling Publishers Private Ltd., New Delhi., 1990

Alexander Paul, *Creativity in small groups,* Sage Publications, Beverly Hills, California, 1982.

Allen Car, "A study of Creativity Training in Elementary Grades in Brazillian Schools", *Dissertation Abstracts International,* December 1974, Vol. 35, No. 6. 3592-A.

Anderson, D. Ronal et al., *Developing Children's Thinking through Science,* Prentice Hall, New Jersey, 1970.

Bernard, O, and Richard.M., *Statistics in Research,* Oxford & IBH Publishing Company, New Delhi, 1975.

Best, J.W. *Research in Education,* Prentice Hall International Ltd., New York, 1963.

Bhaskara.S., *The Effectiveness of Instructional Materials on Verbal Creativity,* Uppal Publishing House, New Delhi, 1990.

Biles, Bertram Robert, "Creative Problem - Solving for Graduate and Professional Students", *Dissertation Abstracts International,* January 1977, Vol. 37, No. 7 , 4220-A.

Brady.L., *Models and Methods of Teaching,* Prentice Hall of Australia Private Ltd., 1985.

Broota, K.D., *Experimental Design in Behavioural Research,* Willey Eastern Ltd., New Delhi, 1989.

Buch, M.B. (Ed.), *Second Survey of Research in Education, (1972 - 1978)*, Society of Educational Research and Development, Baroda, 1978.

Buch, M.B.(Ed.), *Third Survey of Research in Education, (1978 - 1983)*, N.C.E.R.T., New Delhi, 1986.

Buch, M.B.(Ed.), *Fourth Survey of Research in Education, (1983 - 1988)*, N.C.E.R.T., New Delhi, 1991.

Chadha, P.C., et al., *Teaching of Science*, Prakash Brothers, Ludhiana, 1979.

Dayton,C.M., *The Design of Educational Experiments*, Mc.Graw Hill Book Co., London, 1970.

De Bono, *Lateral Thinking - A text Book of Creativity*, Ward Lock Educational Ltd., London, 1970.

Edwards, A.L., *Experimental Design in Psychological Research*, Halt, Rinehart and Winston, Inc., New York 1972.

Edwards, A.L., *Statistical Methods for the Behavioural Sciences*, Halt, Rinehart and Winston, Inc., New York 1963.

Federee, W.T., *Experimental Design*, Oxford and IBH Publishing Co., Calcutta, 1967.

Ferguson, A. George, *Statistical Analysis in Psychology and Education*, Mc.Graw Hill, Kogakush Ltd., New Delhi, 1976.

Fifth Survey of Research Educational Research, (1988 -92) - *Trend Reports*, Vol. I, N.C.E.R.T. , New Delhi, 1997.

Garrette, H.E., *Statistics in Psychology and Education*, Vakils Feffer and Simons Ltd., Bombay, 1981.

Garewal.A., *A Study of Hypothesis Making and Hypothesis Testing Abilities in Science in Relation to Intelligence, Creativity and Socioeconomic Status*, Ph.D. Thesis, M.S. University, Baroda, 1981.

Ghosh, B.N., *Lectures on Scientific Method,* Sterling Publishers Private Ltd., 1986.

Gordon, J.J. William, *Synectics: The Development of Creative Capacity,* Harper and Row Publishers, New York, 1961.

.... Government of India, *Indian Education Commission Report (1964 - 1966),* Ministry of Education, New Delhi, 1966.

...... Government of India, *National Policy in Education,* 1986, M.H.R.D., New Delhi, 1986.

Guilford, J.P., *Fundamental Statistics in Psychology and Education,* Mc.Graw Hill Book Company, London, 1956.

Johnson, O.G. and Bommarito, J.W. *Tests and Measurements in Child Development: A Handbook,* Josses - Bass Inc., Publishers, San Francisco, 1971.

Joyce Bruce and Weil Marsha, *Models of Teaching,* Prentice Hall of India Private Ltd., New Delhi, 1990.

Kerlinger, F.N. , *Foundations of Behavioural Research,* Holt, Rinehart and Winston, Inc., New York, 1964.

Khatena, Joe., Abstract of Analogy Strategies and the production of original verbal Images, *The Journal of Creative Behaviour,* New York, Vol. II, No.3, Third Quarter, 1977.

Kleinmuntz Benjamin, *Problem Solving - Research, Method and Theory,* John Wiley and Sons, New York, 1966.

Koul, Lokesh, *Methodology of Educational Research,* Vani Educational Books, New Delhi, 1984.

Kusuma.A., *Creativity and Cognitive Styles in Children,* Discovery Publishing House, New Delhi, 1977.

Lindquist, E.F., *Design and Analysis of Experiment in Psychology and Education*, Houghton, Mifflin Co., Boston, 1953.

Murrey John, *The Teaching of General Science*, - A report by General science subcommittee of the Science Master's Association, John Murrey Publishers Ltd., 1960.

.... *National Policy on Education - 1986*, Government of India, M.H.R.D., New Delhi 1986.

Nathan. S. Washton, *Teaching Science Creatively*, W.B. Saunders Company, London 1967.

Nayak, A.K. and Singh, K.Uttan, *Science Education*, Commonwealth Publishers, New Delhi, 1997.

Norman, R.F. Maier, *Problem Solving and Creativity in Individual and Groups*, Wadsworth Publishing Company, California, 1970.

Olton, Robert M., 'The Development of Productive Thinking Skills in fifth grade children', *Dissertation Abstracts International*, September 1977, Vol. 38, No. 3., 1214 - A.

Peter. W.M.J. , *Statistical Design and Analysis of Experiments*, The MacMillan Co., New York 1971.

Raina, M.K.(Ed.), *Creativity Research - International Perspective*, N.C.E.R.T., New Delhi, 1990.

Raven, J.C. Court, J.H. and Raven.J., *Manual for Ravens's Progressive Matrices Vocabulary Scales*, (Standard Progressive Matrices), Lewis and Company Ltd., London. H.K., 1988.

.... *Report of University Education Commission* (1948 - 49) Vol. 1, Ministry of Education, Government of India, Delhi, 1962.

.... *Report of Secondary Education Commission*, Ministry of Education, Government of India, Delhi, 1962.

Sanders, H.D., *Statistics—A Fresh Approach,* McGraw Hill Publishing Company, New York, 1990.

Sansanwal, D.N. and Josh, A., *Manual for Test of Higher Mental Ability in Science (THMAS),* National Psychological Corporation, Agra, 1989.

Sharma, H.L., *School Science Education in India,* Common Wealth Publishers, New Delhi, 1989.

Sharma, R.C., *Modern Science Teaching,* Dhanpat Rai and Sons, Delhi, Jullunder, 1992.

Seigal, *Non Parametric Statistics for Behavioural Sciences,* Mc.Graw Hill, New York, 1956.

Siddiqui, M.H. and Khan.M.S., *Models of Teaching - Theory and Research,* Ashish Publishing House, New Delhi, 1991.

Simonds, Doris A.G., Stimulating Creativity Learning by Analogy in Student-Centered Undergraduate Science Classes, *Dissertation Abstracts International,* August 1978, Vol. 39, No. 2. 799 - A.

Singh, P., *Instructional Objectives in General Science, Development of Teacher Education,* N.C.E.R.T., New Delhi, 1971.

Smith, James.A. *Setting Conditions for Creative Teaching in Elementary School,* Allyn Bacon, Boston, 1966.

Stein, *Development of Creative Ability,* N.C.E.R.T. New Delhi, 1985.

Swamy, A. Effect of Inquiry Training Model of Teaching Science of Science Process Skills, Creativity and *Curiosity of Secondary School Students,* Ph.D. Thesis, Karnataka University, Dharwad, 1995.

Thurber.A. Walter and Collette, T. Alfred, Teaching Science in today's Secondary Schools, Prentice Hall of India, New Delhi, 1964.

Torrance. E.P. and Torrance, J.P., 'Future Problem Solving:

National Interscholastic Competition and Curriculum Project', *Journal of Creative Behaviour*, Vol. 12. No. 2 II Wuarter, 87 - 89, 1978.

Tripathi, S.N. *Talent and Creativity*, Print Palace, Agra, 1996.

Tuckman, B,W., *Conducting Educational Research*, Harcourt Brace Jovanovich Inc., New York, 1978.

Twiss, Ransom George, *Science Teaching*, The Macmillan Company, New York, 1925.

.... *UNESCO Source Book for Science Teaching*, Oxford and IBH Publishing Company, New Delhi, 1971.

Vaidya Narendra, *Impact of Science Teaching*, Oxford and I.B.H. Publishing Company, New Delhi, 1971.

Walker, H.M. and Lev. J., 'Statistical Inference', Oxford and IBH Publishing Co., Calcutta, 1965.

Weil Marsha, Joyce Bruce and Kluwin bridget, *Personal Models of Teaching - Expanding you:: teaching Repertoire*, Printice Hall, Inc., Englewood Cliffs, New Jersey, 1978.

Websites:
www.Excite.com
www.Yahoo.com
www.google.com
www.univr.it
www.cte.usf.edn
www.sfsu.edu
www.synecticsworld.com

Index

❑❑❑